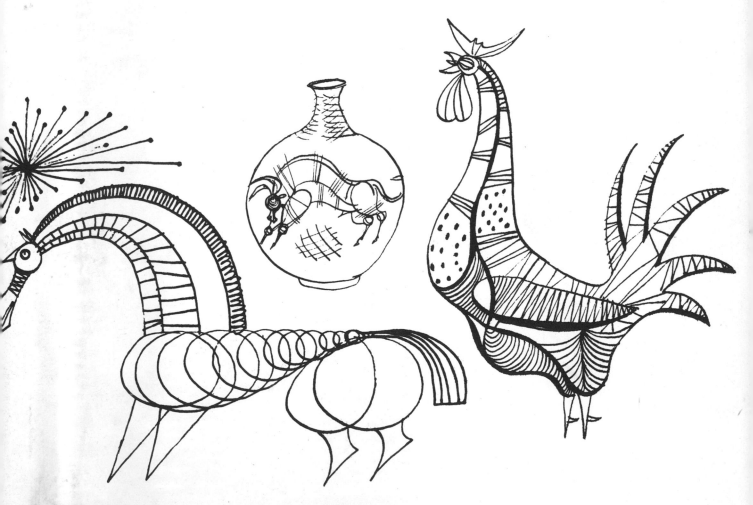

AARON BOHROD  a pottery sketchbook

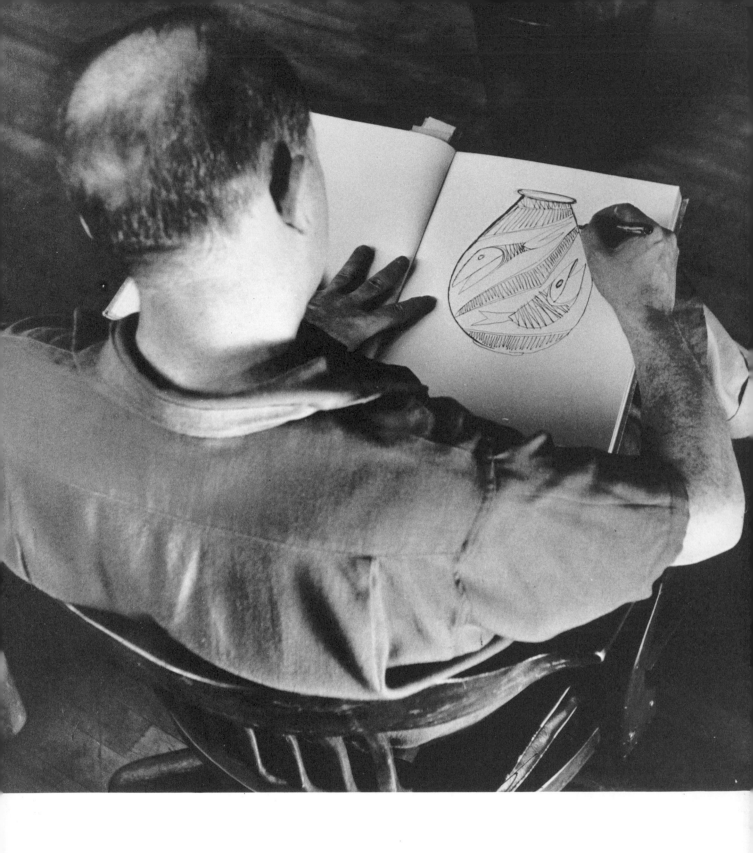

Aaron Bohrod

a pottery sketchbook

The University of Wisconsin Press, *Madison*, 1959

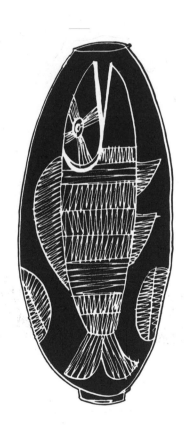

TO CARLTON BALL

*F. Carlton Ball (left) and Aaron Bohrod (right)
working together in Mr. Ball's workshop,
Carbondale, Illinois, 1954.*

*From four of his large pottery sketchbooks
averaging about 9 inches by 12 inches
in size, Aaron Bohrod selected the pottery
drawings reproduced on the following
pages. The average reduction for full-page
drawings was about 20 per cent.*

PREFACE The sketch has often been deemed an artist's revelation of what lies nearest his heart. Free from the rationalized embroidery he weaves to dress up his finished art product whether that be a painting, sculpture, or an object of one of the decorative arts, the sketch is the artist's naked plan: the soul of his aesthetic concept.

Ingres has been quoted as saying: "Drawing is the probity of art." And the unaffected honesty of the artist's sketch has sometimes led to a closer understanding of his purpose and his stature than the more complete but at times obscured statements which constitute the final work.

An artist's sketchbook is his storehouse of ideas. Into its pages he pours his dreams, his stray and idle notions, his useful and useless doodles, his

"Self-Portrait:
The Art of Painting"
9 by 12 inches
1958

plans for further explorations. The entire basic program in which his art is rooted may be found on these humble sheets of paper. An artist may use his sketchbook for the trial of alternate versions of a work he expects to bring to completion in another medium or for the pure joy of executing the drawing itself: the sketch for the sketch's sake.

In this book a sampling of pages has been extracted from my sketchbooks which pertains peculiarly to my work in pottery. A special series of this kind of drawing came into being when my first works in this decorative art became enmeshed in coöperative effort with the ceramic artist F. Carlton Ball, now at the University of Southern California. In 1950, when Ball taught on the campus of the University of Wisconsin, a tentative collaboration began. This comprised Ball's throwing of pottery at the wheel and my attempt to extend his work decoratively. The collaboration has blossomed over the years to a continuing though intermittent exchange of ideas and mutual creation. The intermittent nature of our work has been necessitated by the existing distance between our several campuses of operation. Of course the actual production of pottery can only go forward when we are to-

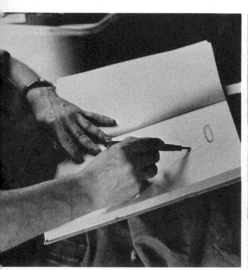

"Wooden Rock"
16 by 12 inches
1955

Pen, brush, and scratching
point in the hands
of the artist produced
the variety of designs and
embellishments illustrated
below. The objects of the
Bohrod-Ball Collaboration
tend to be large in size,
with the average about 16
or 18 inches high. The torso
vases and some of the larger
urns are 2 or 3 feet high.

gether in one workshop. But the collaboration – irregular as it is—continues, and the sketchbook pages mount up with more ideas than can possibly be executed. To date, perhaps five hundred individual pieces of pottery have been inscribed with both our signatures and it is hoped that many more will eventually come into existence.

The sketchbook is the life blood of the pottery collaboration. From its pages Ball makes selections of ideas or of particular shapes so that these forms may be furnished for completion. Or on forms of his own devising I will translate ideas just hinted at or firmly established in my books to fit the needs of the particular pot under consideration. There is usually no intermediate drawing necessary.

I have always believed that the most interesting decorated pot is one which when turned in the hands will show in its decorative aspects mutual relation of all its parts and with the form as a whole. Inventive variety held within the framework of the general scheme makes rewarding the views of the pot's entire surface. So, as may be seen on some of these pages, I prepare myself with more than enough variations of the basic thought that selection may be made for final use of the best

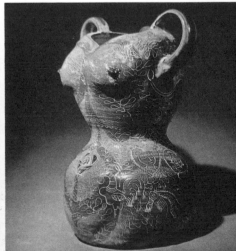

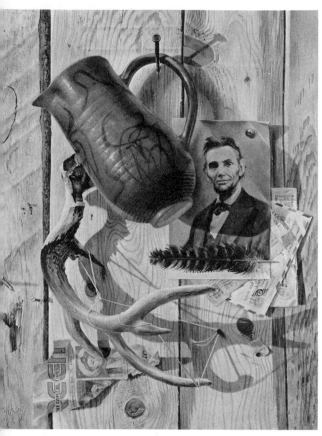

and most fitting material. No matter how much preparation has been made, when confronted with the actual piece of pottery to be worked on, changes must take place to comply with the demands of the form. But the dry run of the drawing itself makes these adjustments a simple matter.

Design based on natural form is a recurrent theme on these pages. With the easily retained basic forms of horse, fish, and bird, great and unexpected departures can be made from these symbols while still communicating the recognizable image. For instance, with the simple fish it seems impossible to exhaust the invention this basic natural form offers. In this connection a knowledge of the construction and anatomy of the animals and of the human figures sometimes used is of importance in giving a ring of authority to even the most radical of departures from actual appearance. Of infinite possibility and variety too may be the secondary decorative elements related in feeling to the main motif and utilized for bridging gaps between the principal elements.

The fantasies, abstract devices, and diverting variations on the promptings of nature serve more suitably the creation of a decorative art object than a painting, which, I believe, requires another way

"A Lincoln Portrait"
16 by 20 inches
1954

"Things of This World" (left), 24 by 10 inches, 1956, and "A Row of Things" (below), 19-5/8 by 7-3/8 inches, 1957

The photograph directly below was taken at Mr. Bohrod's studio on the University of Wisconsin campus. Those on the facing page were taken in Mr. Ball's workshop.

of communication. The outpouring of these ideas breeds infinitely more ideas and fantasies and variations. There is no better way to induce the flow of this kind of invention than by recording these thoughts in sketch form. For myself, involved at the moment with a very demanding, incisive way of still-life painting, the lightheartedness of this kind of relaxed conceit offers an outlet to many more than one impulse which is usually brewing inside the artist. Whether or not a sketch ever develops into a finished piece of pottery is not tremendously important. The pen line I usually use in my direct sketchbook work serves as a free-flowing complement to the slowly nurtured paintings I produce. The invented material I employ is also a far cry from the concrete things of the world I use as symbols in my painting. But that makes all the more satisfying the seriously playful expression of the hundreds of whimsical notions that flow from the pen.

June, 1959   Aaron Bohrod

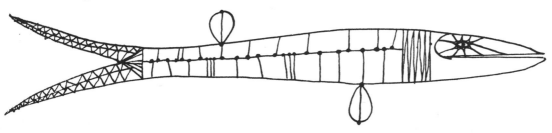

The painting, "Self-Portrait: The Eye and I," used on the
back of the jacket of this book is now a part of the
collection of Mrs. William Hoard of Fort Atkinson,
Wisconsin. It was painted in the diminutive size of 5-3/4
inches square. "Self-Portrait: The Art of Painting" on page
viii is in the collection of Mr. and Mrs. Lawrence Fleischman
of Detroit, Michigan, and "Wooden Rock" on page ix is
in the collection of Mr. and Mrs. William J. Poplack of
Birmingham, Michigan. On page x, the original of "A
Lincoln Portrait" is in the collection of Professor and Mrs.
Harry Steenbock of Madison, Wisconsin. "A Row of Things"
on page xi is in the collection of Dr. and Mrs. Albert Ellis,
New York City, and "Things of This World" on the same
page is in the collection of Mr. and Mrs. Robert Levine,
Madison, Wisconsin. The photographs of the artist's
hands on pages viii and ix and the frontispiece were
taken by Conrad Brown, Editor of Craft Horizons.

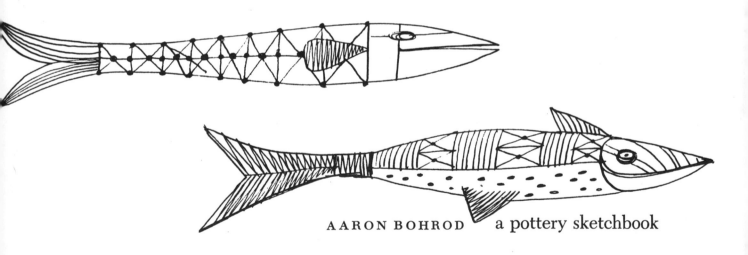

AARON BOHROD   a pottery sketchbook

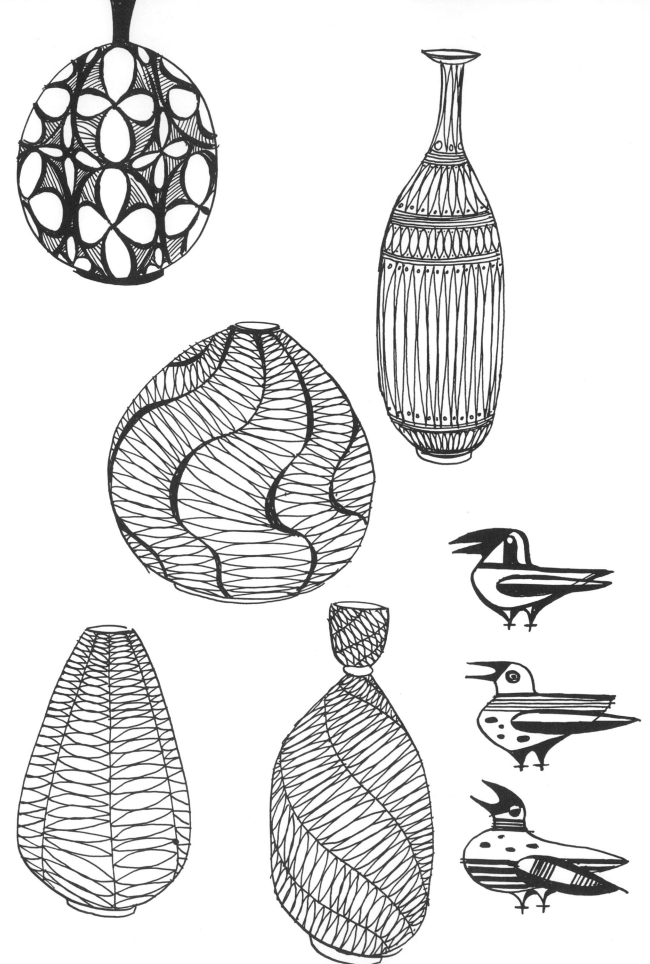

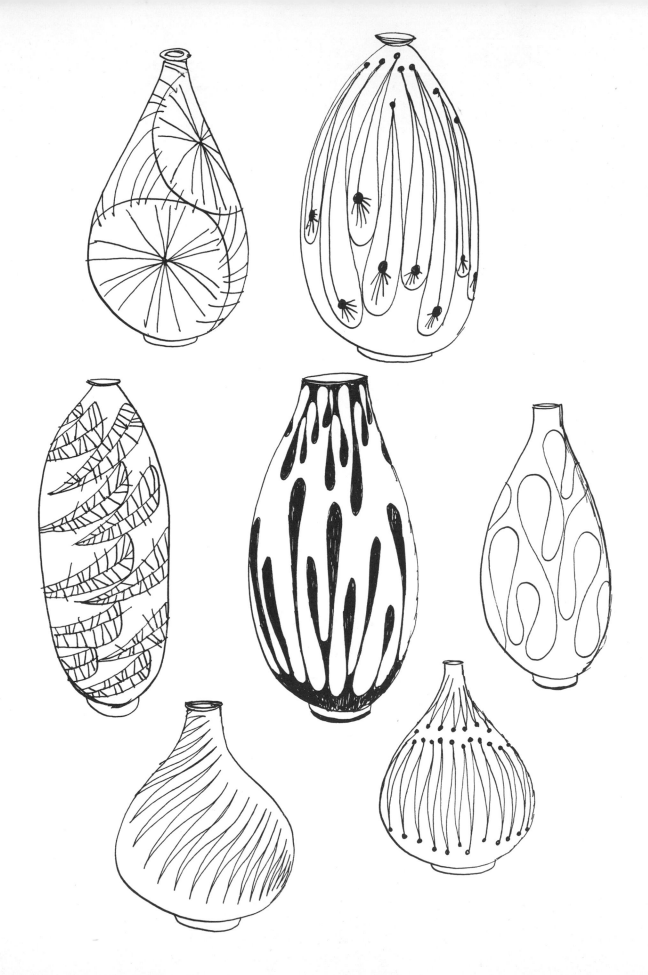

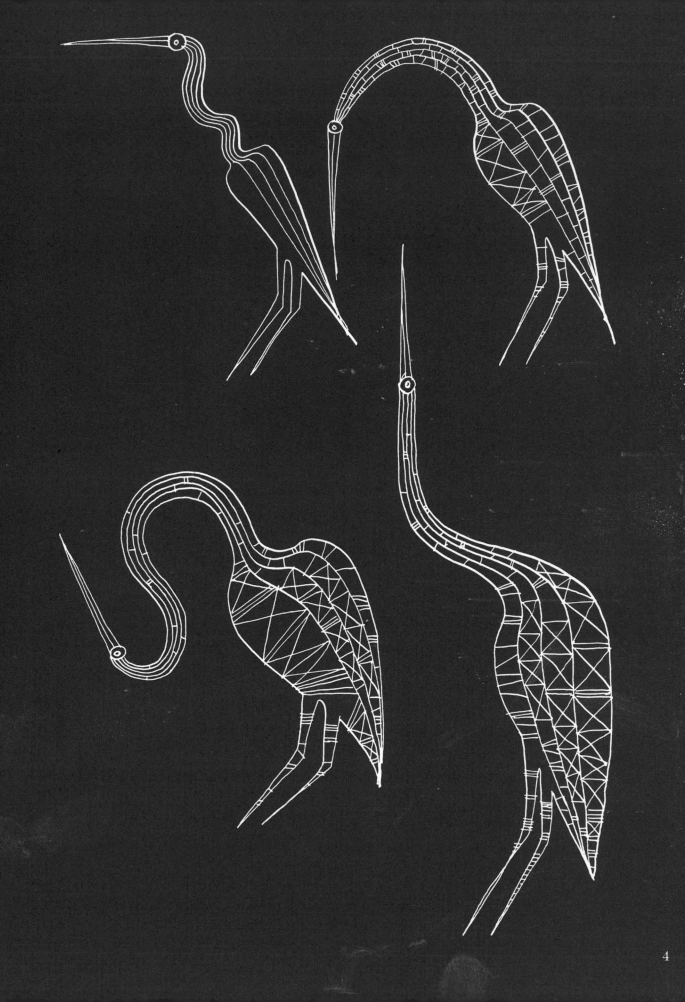

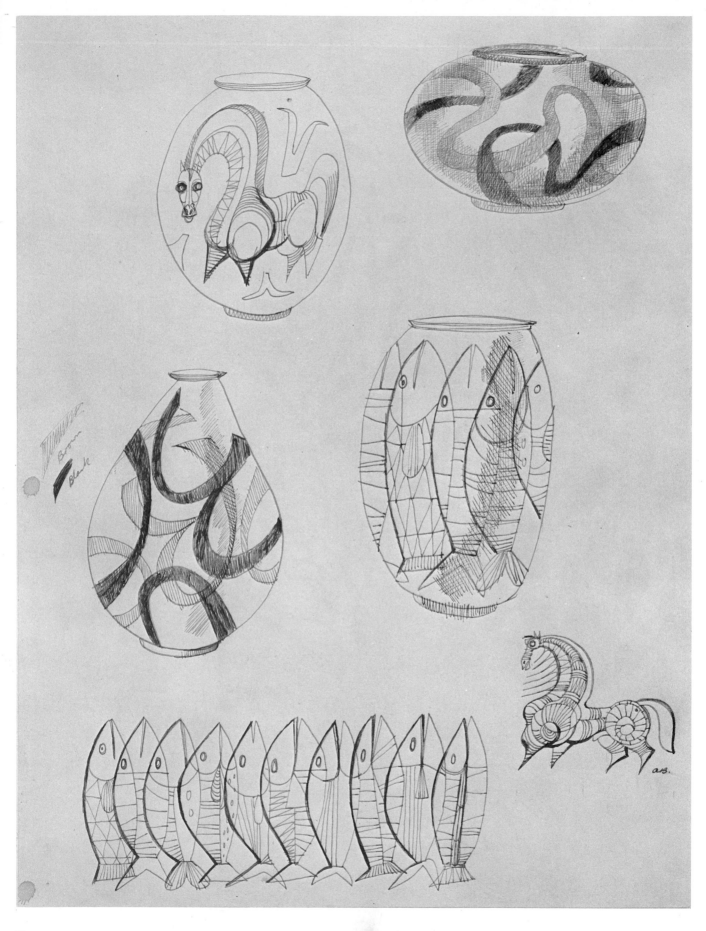

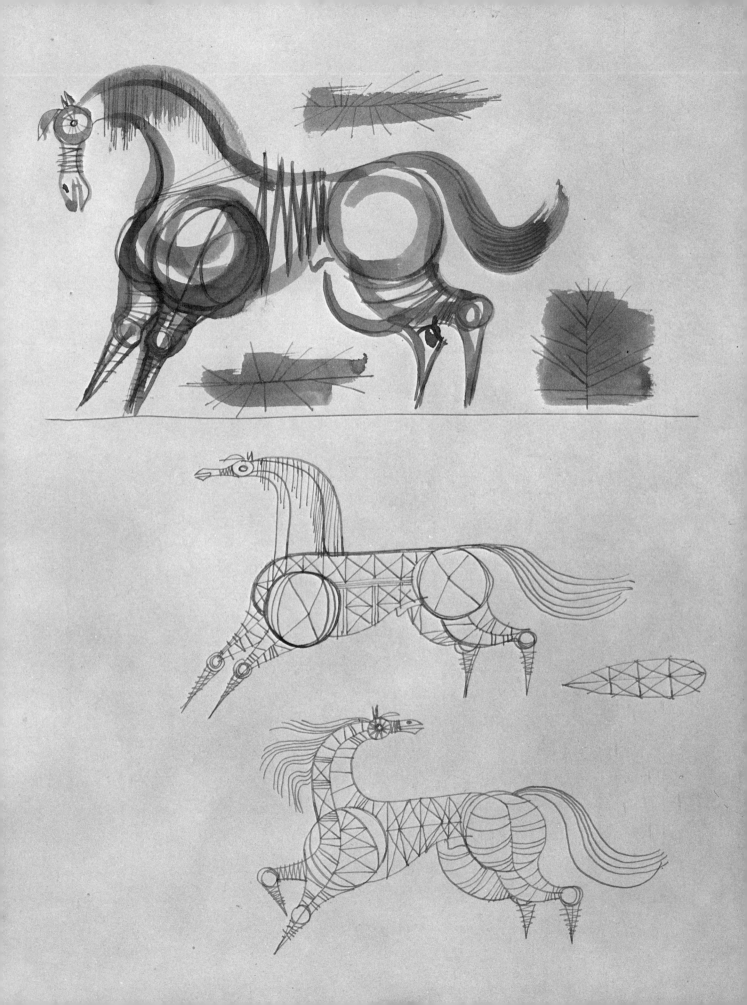

10

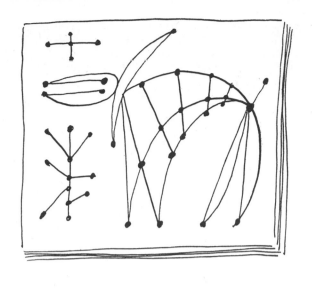

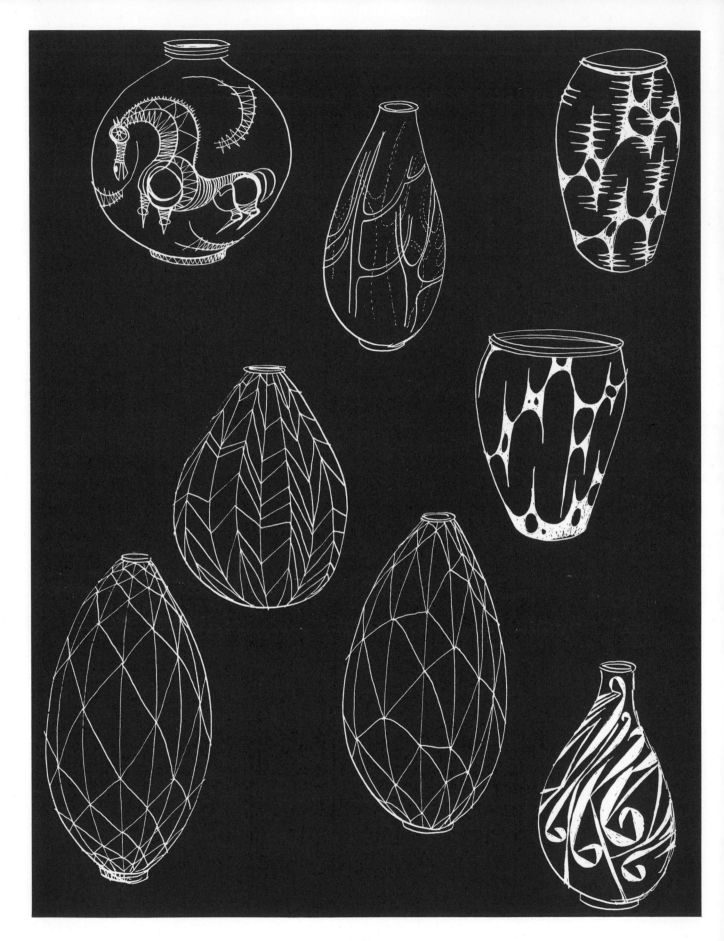

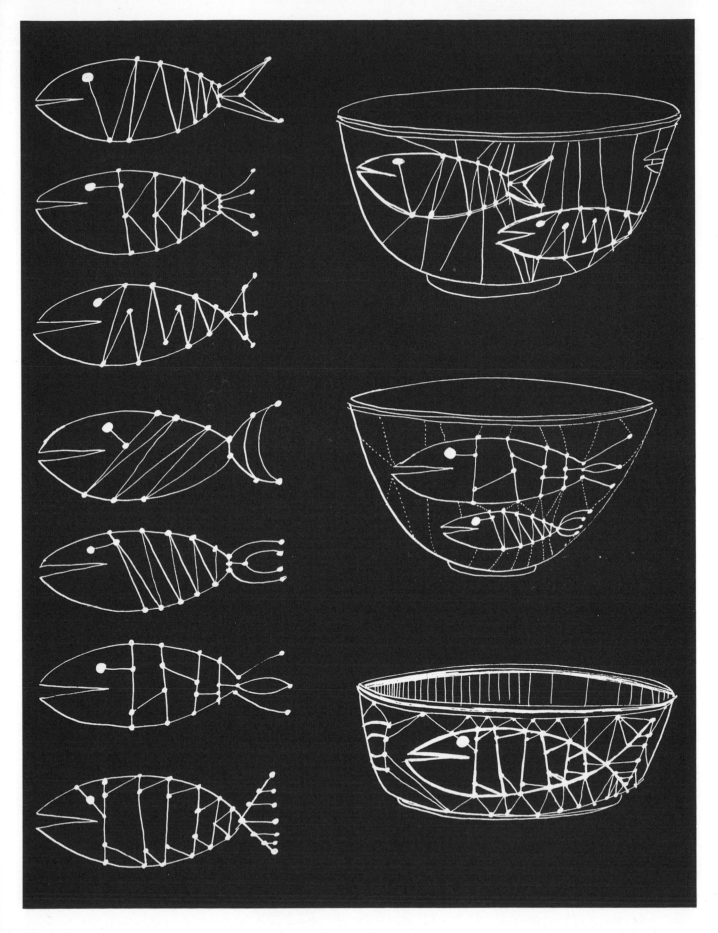

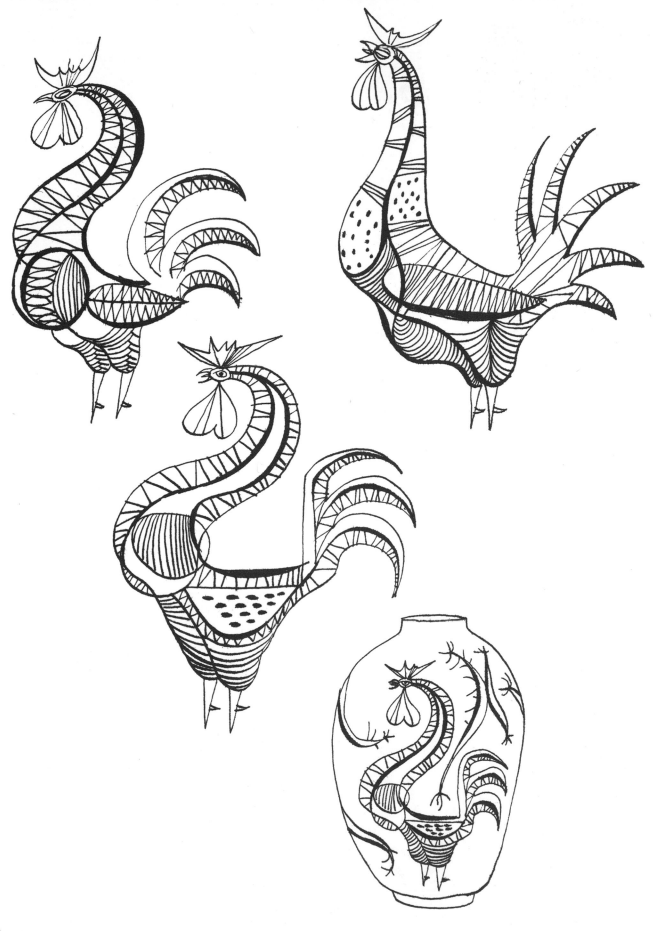

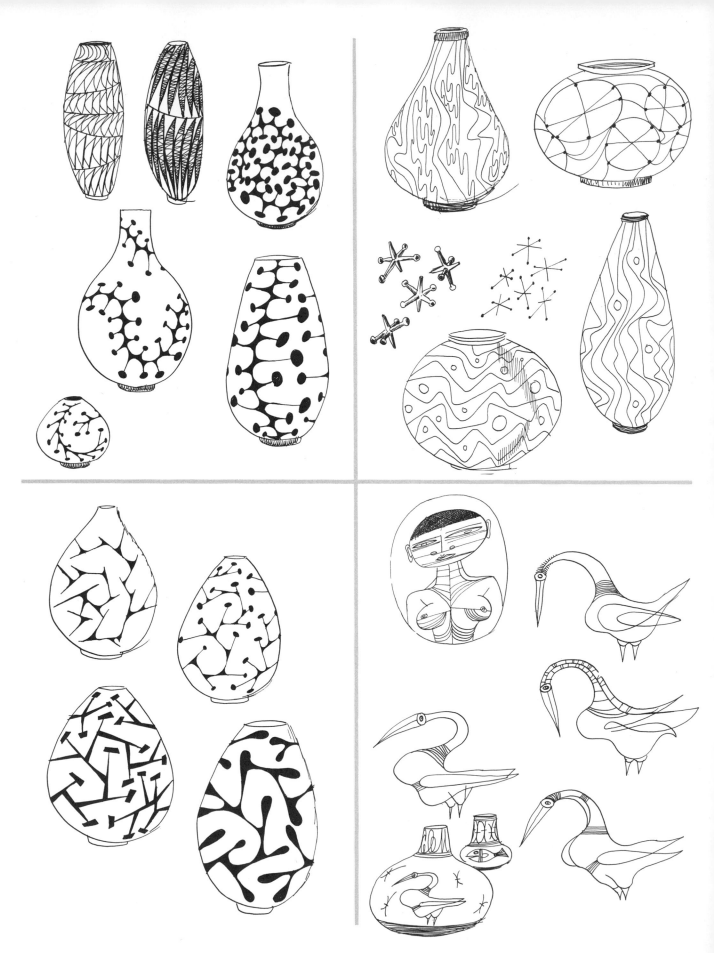

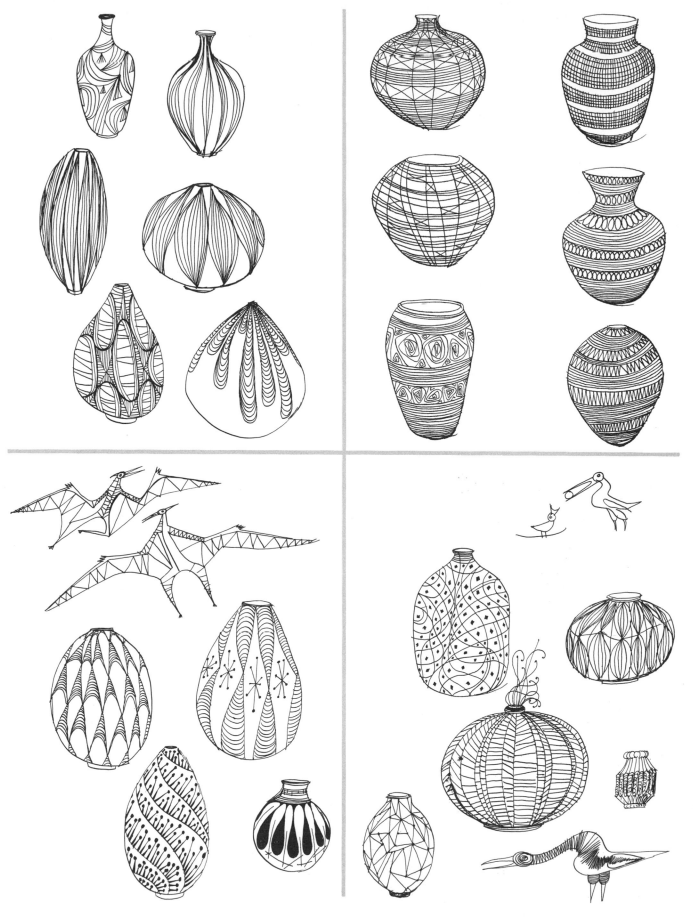

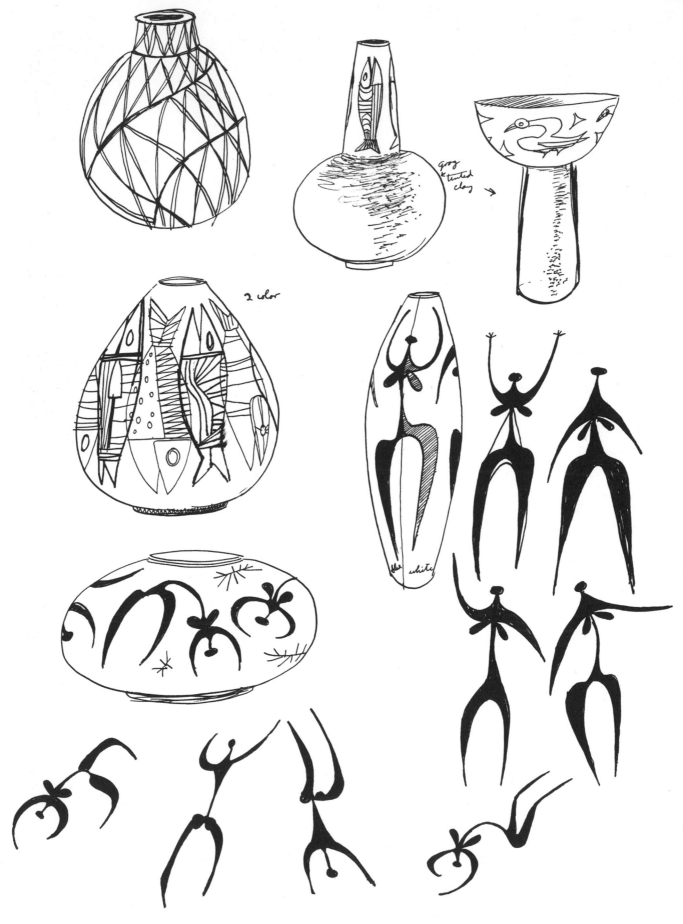

grey
& tinted
clay →

2 color

blue white

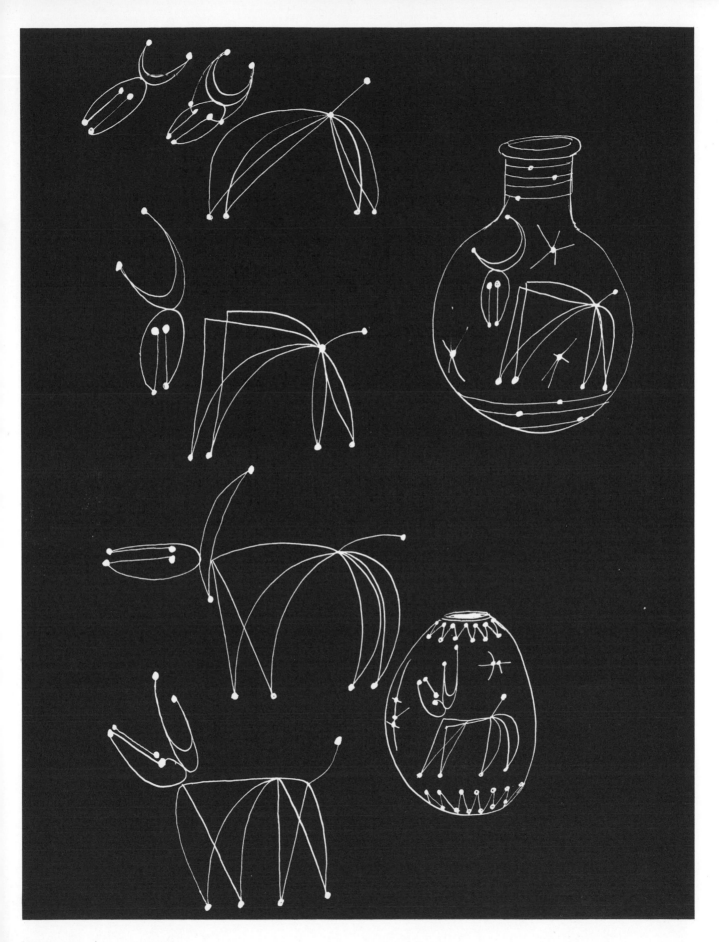

21

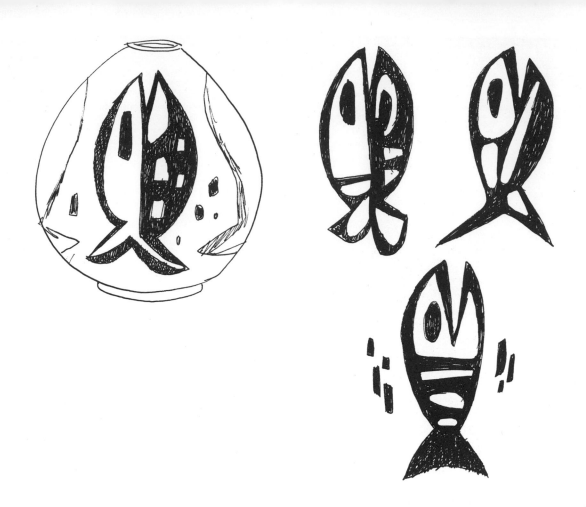

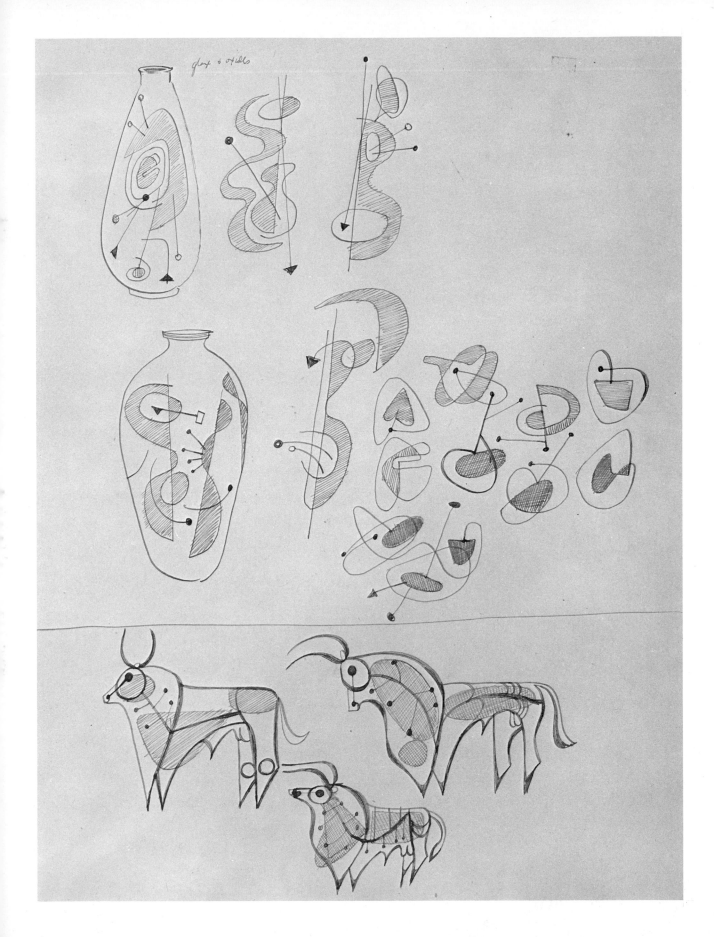

glaze & oxides

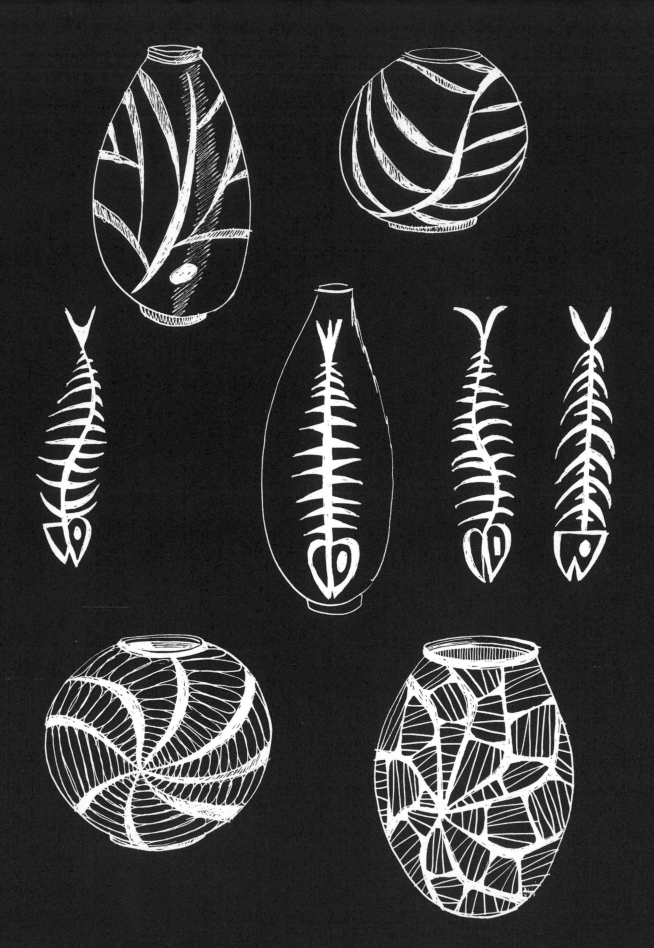

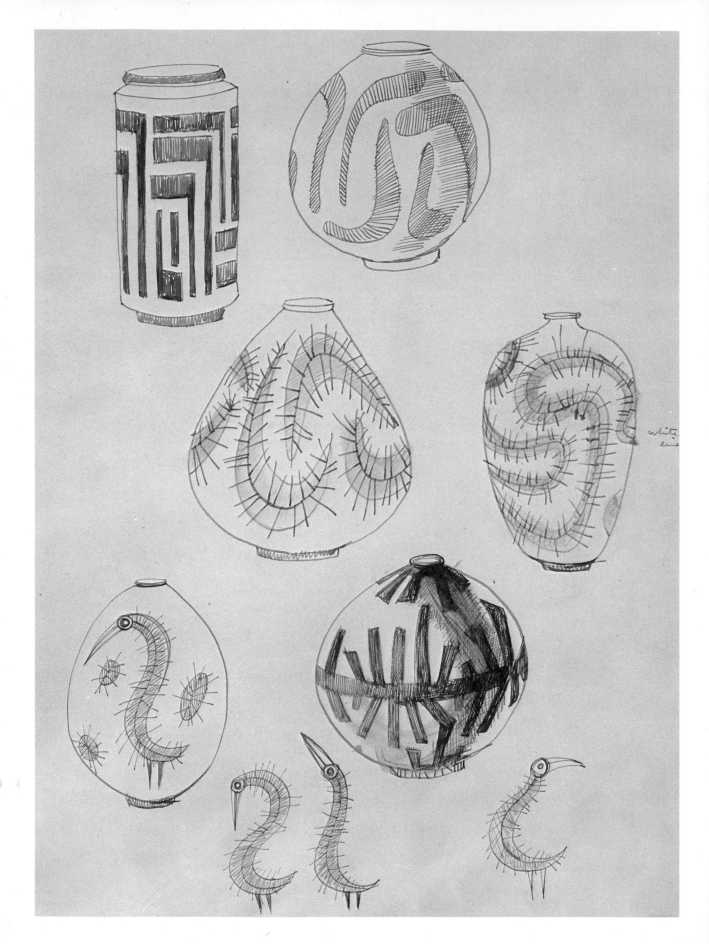

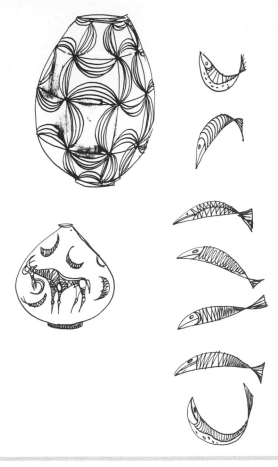

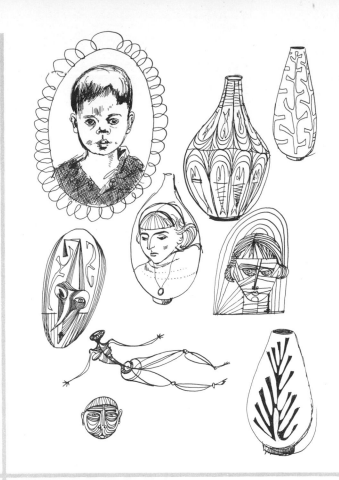

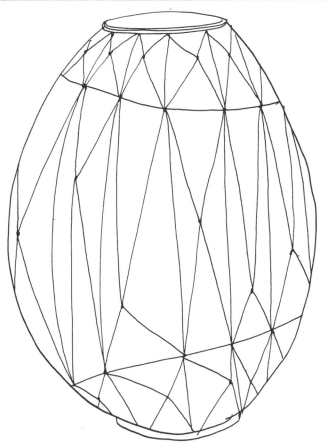

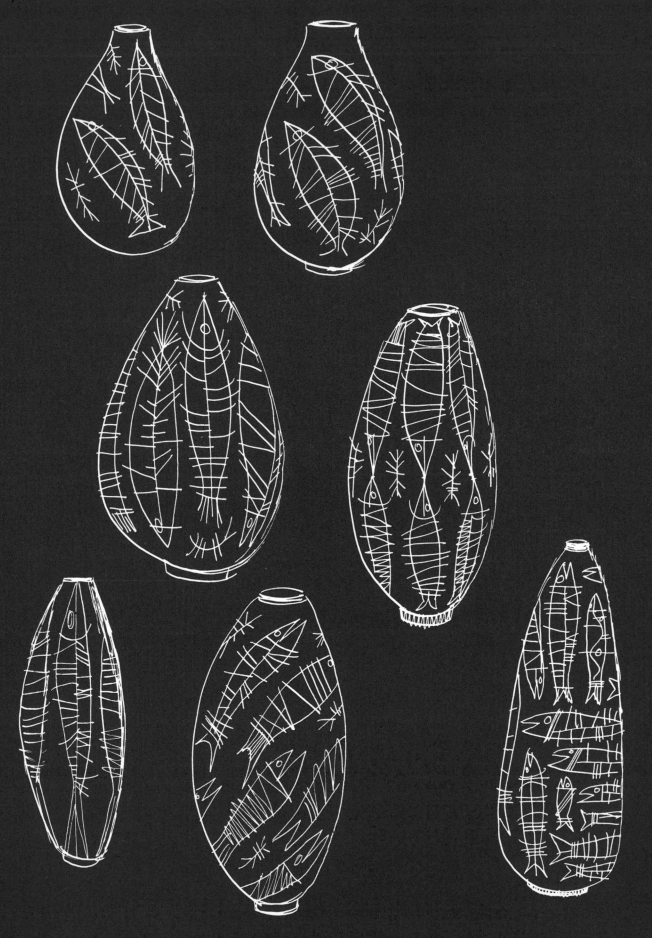

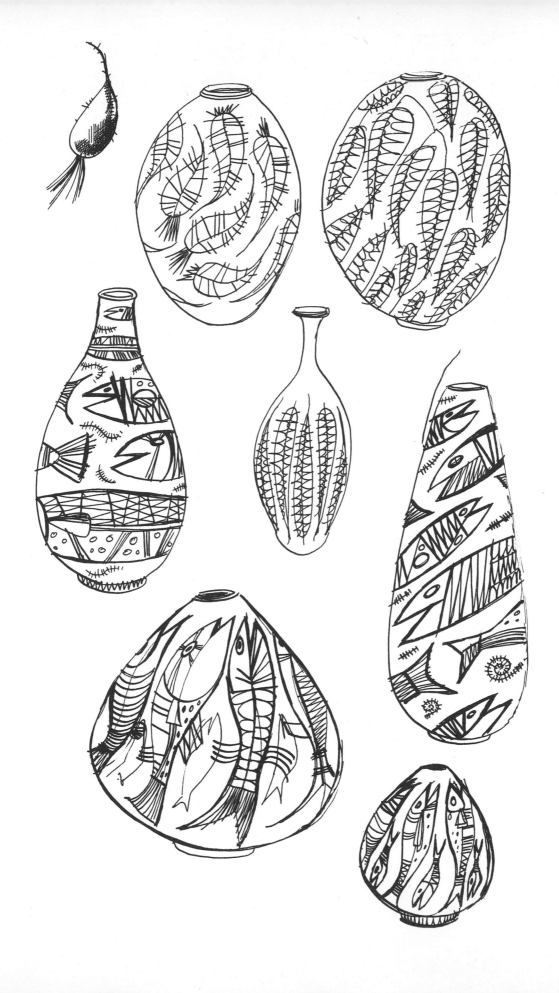

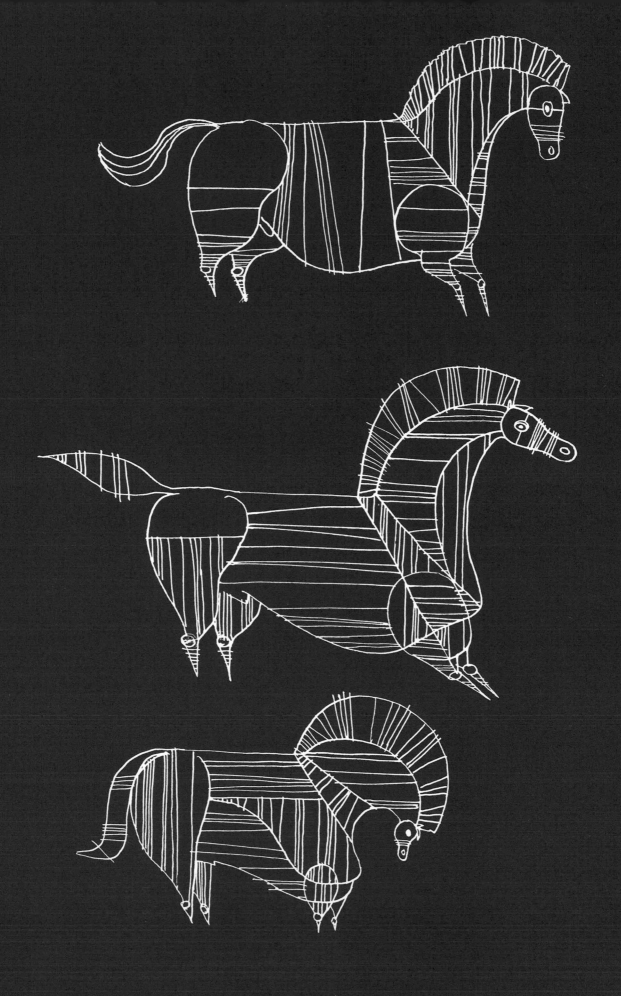

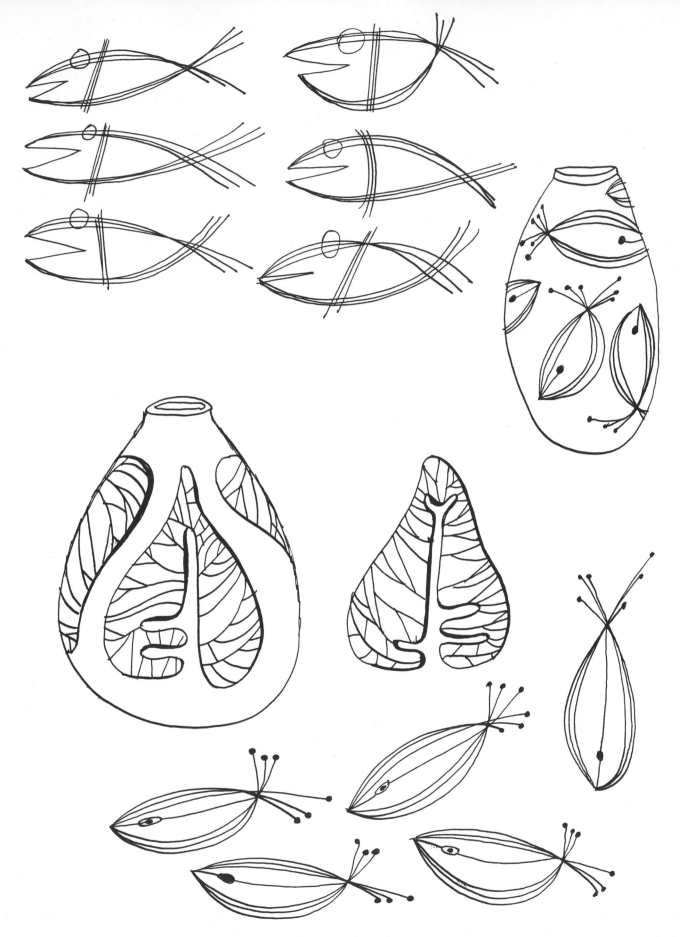

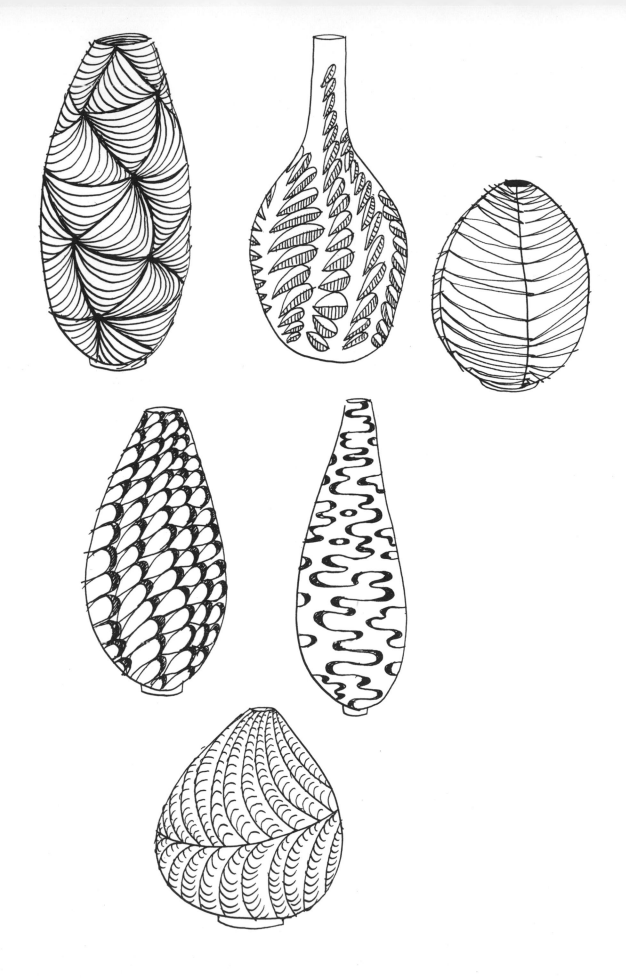

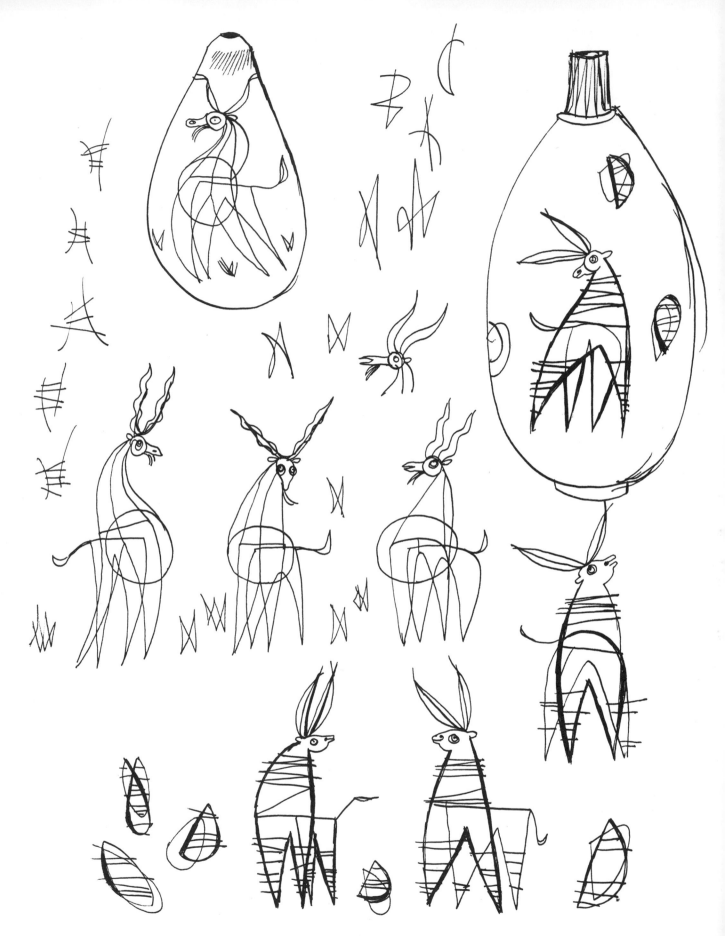

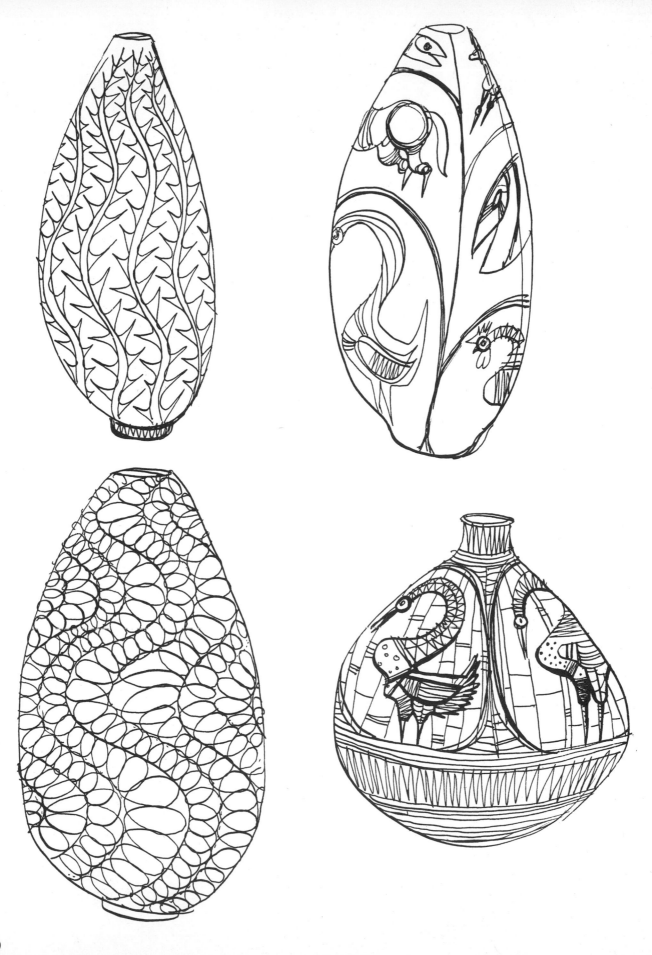

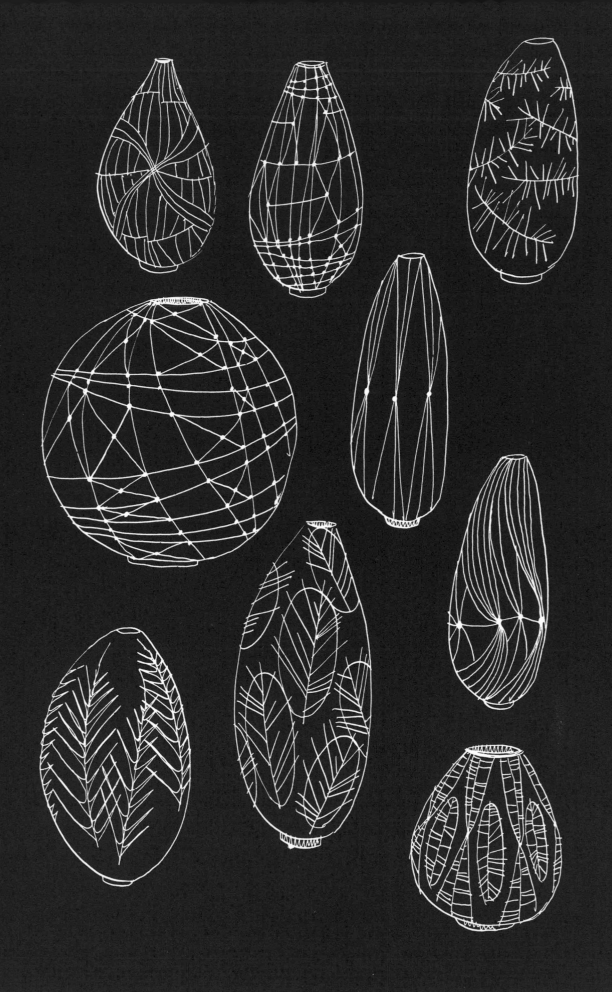

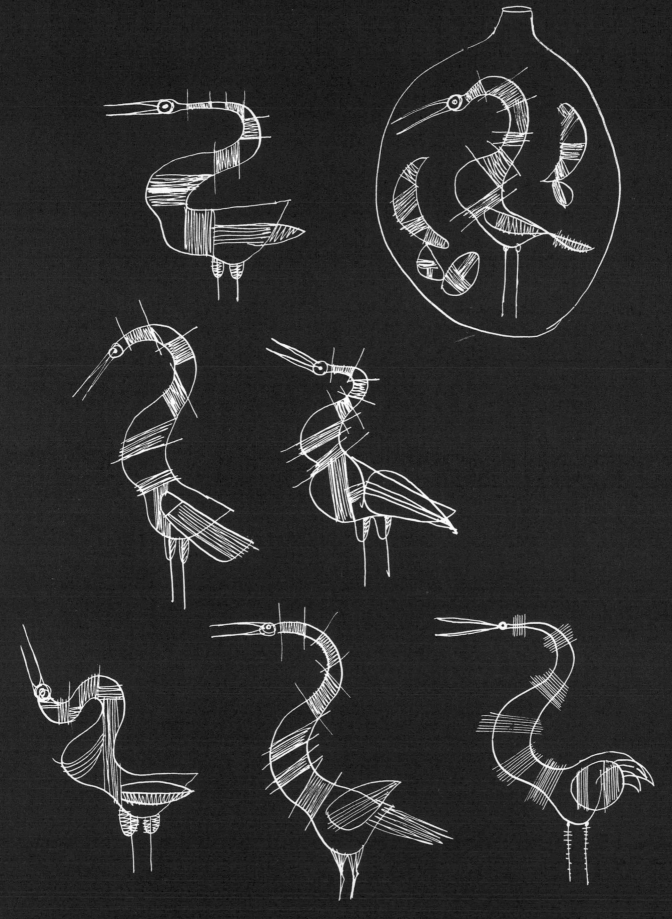

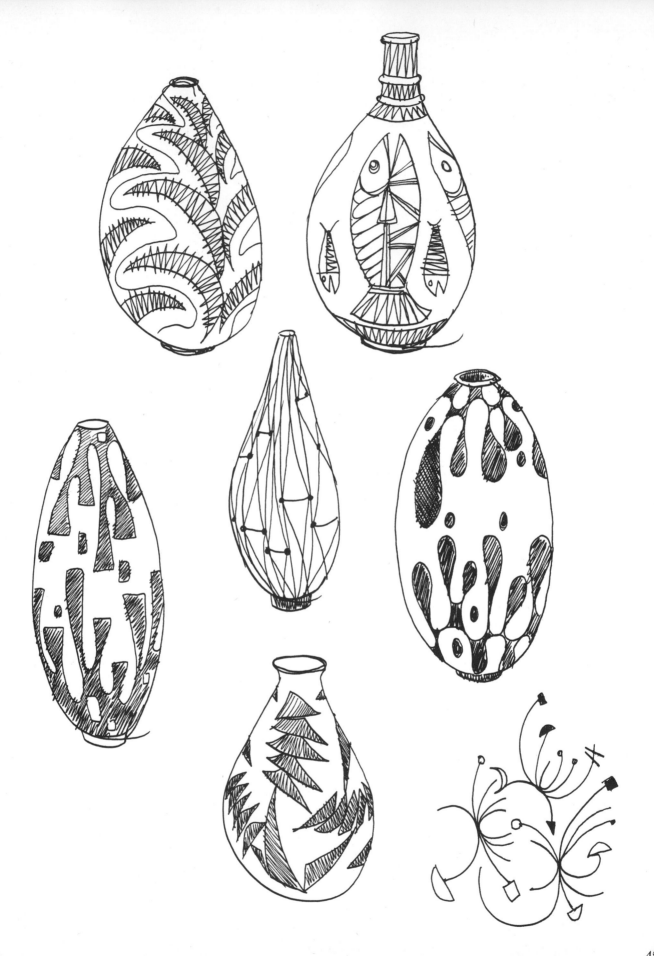

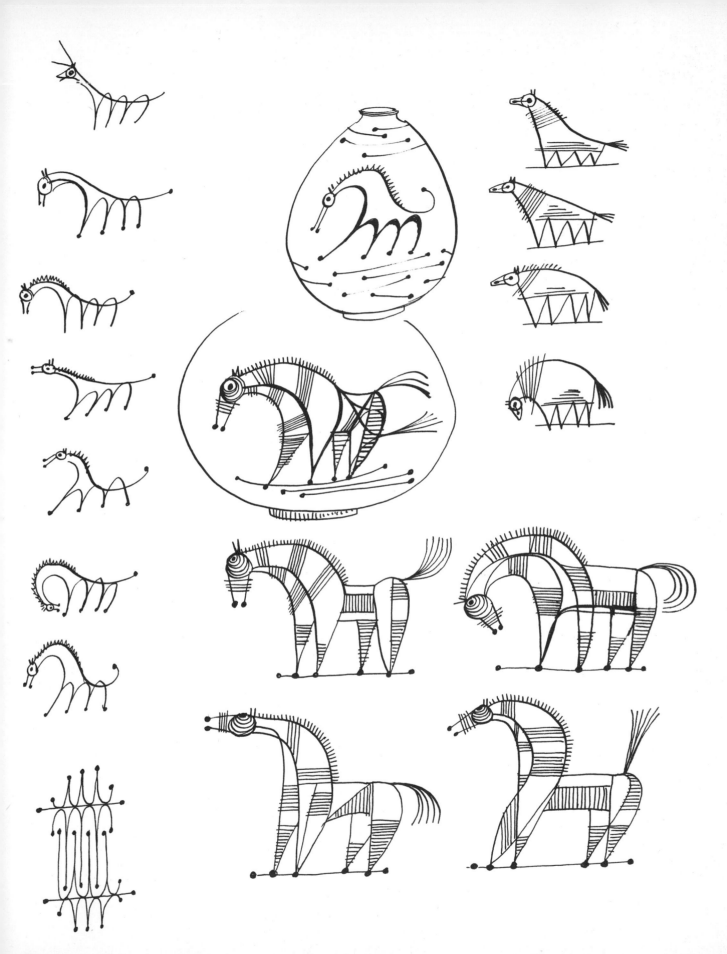

43

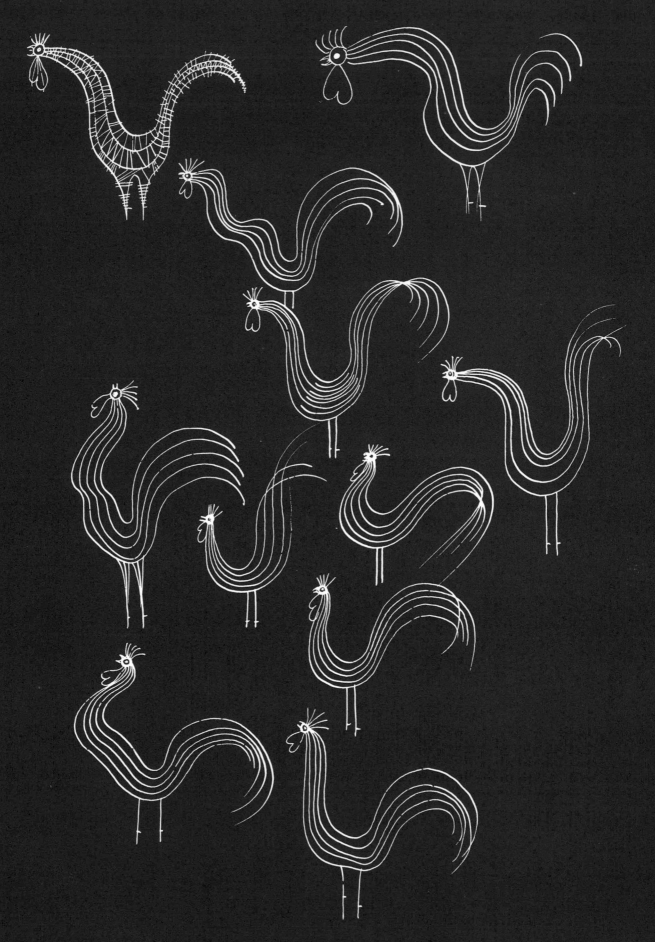

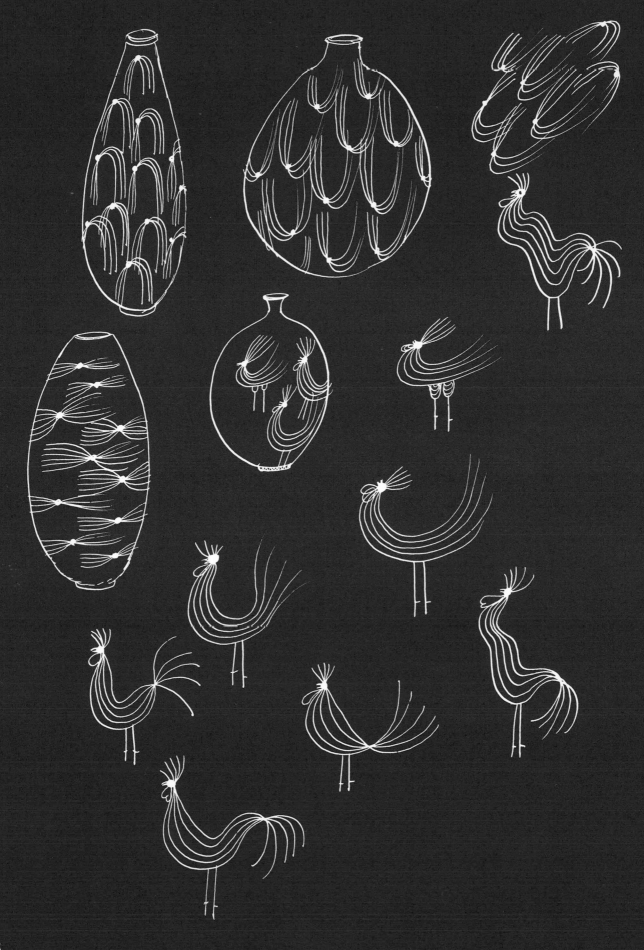

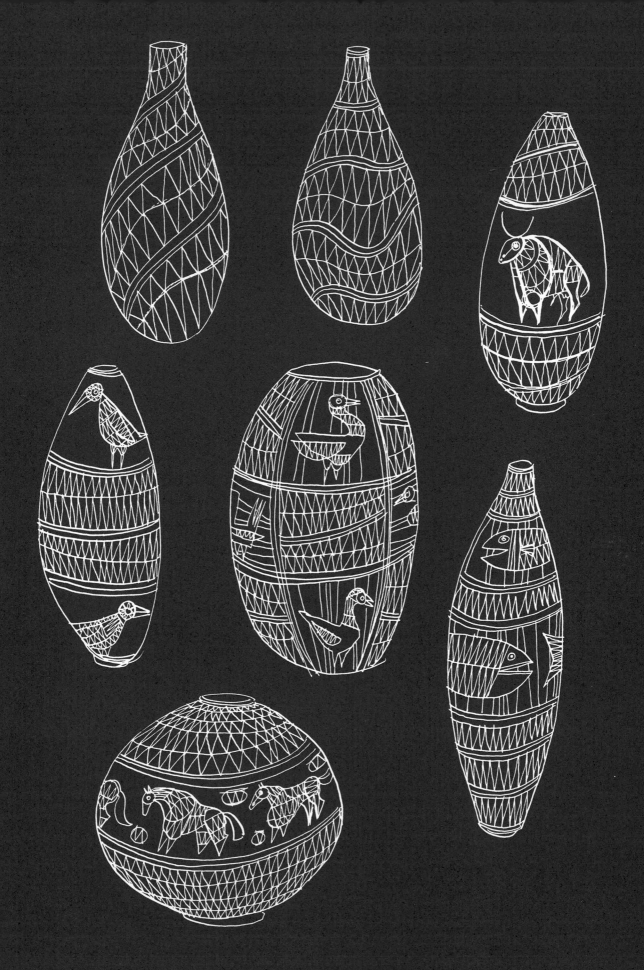

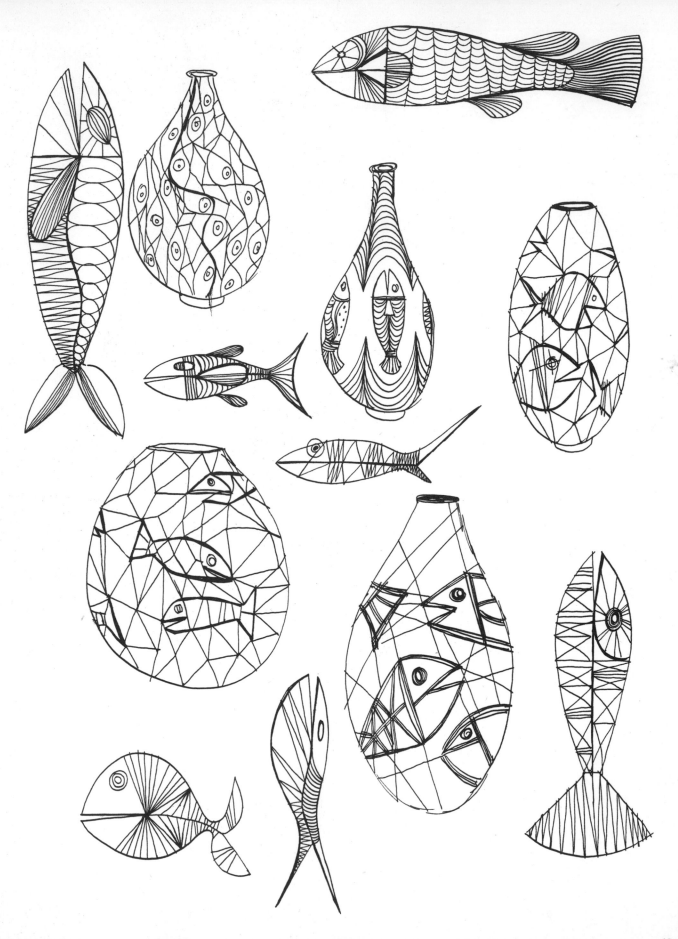

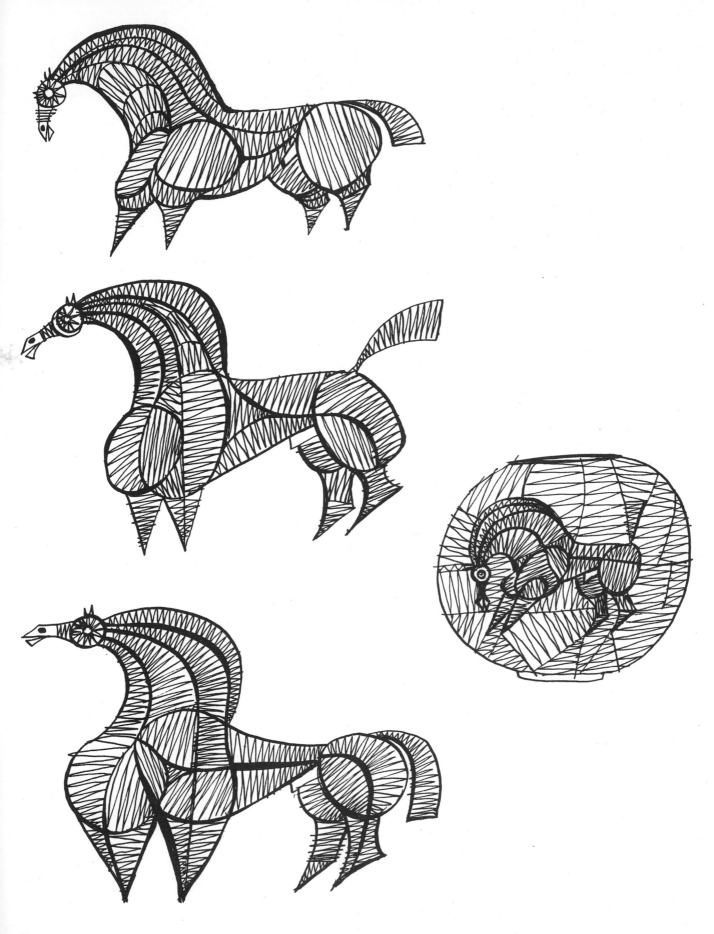

49

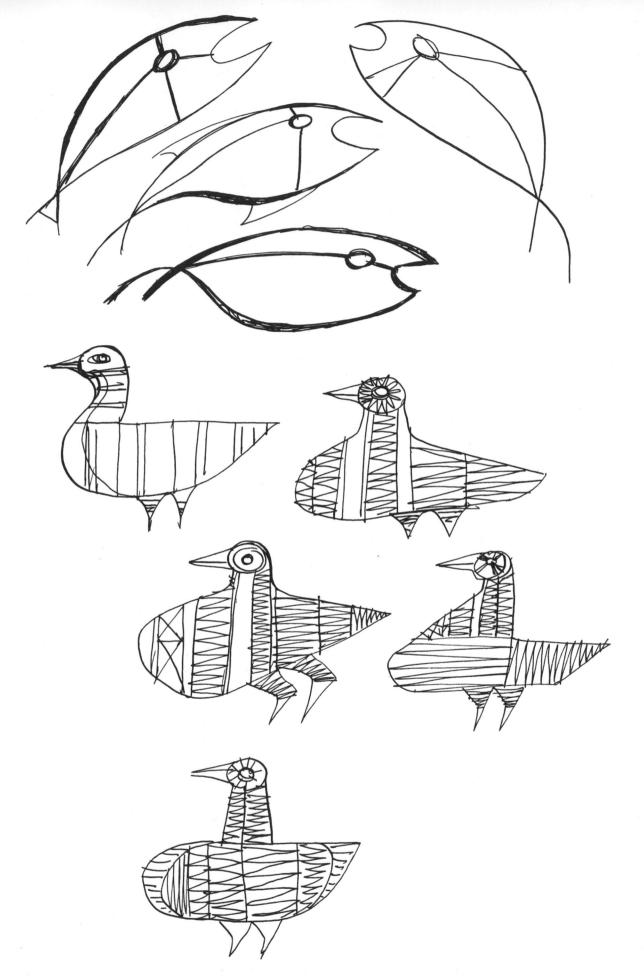

53

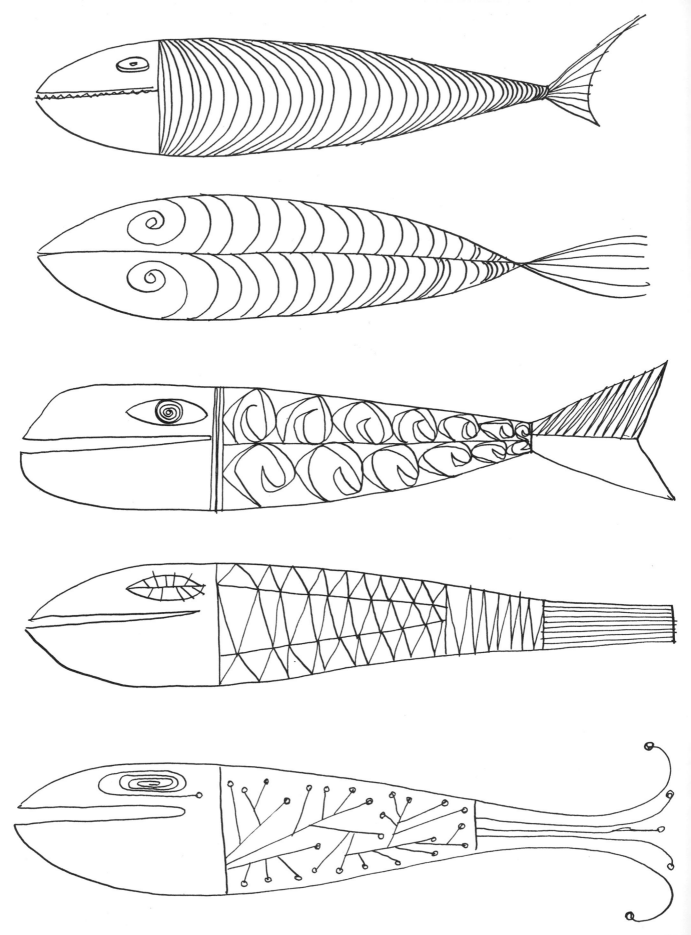

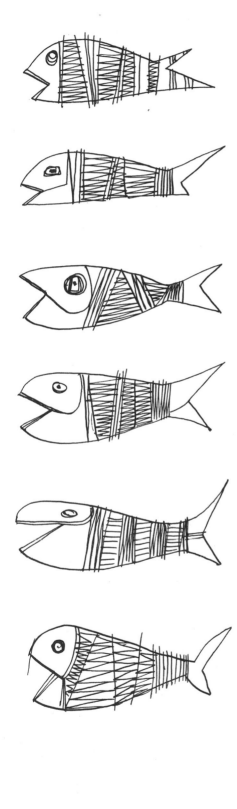

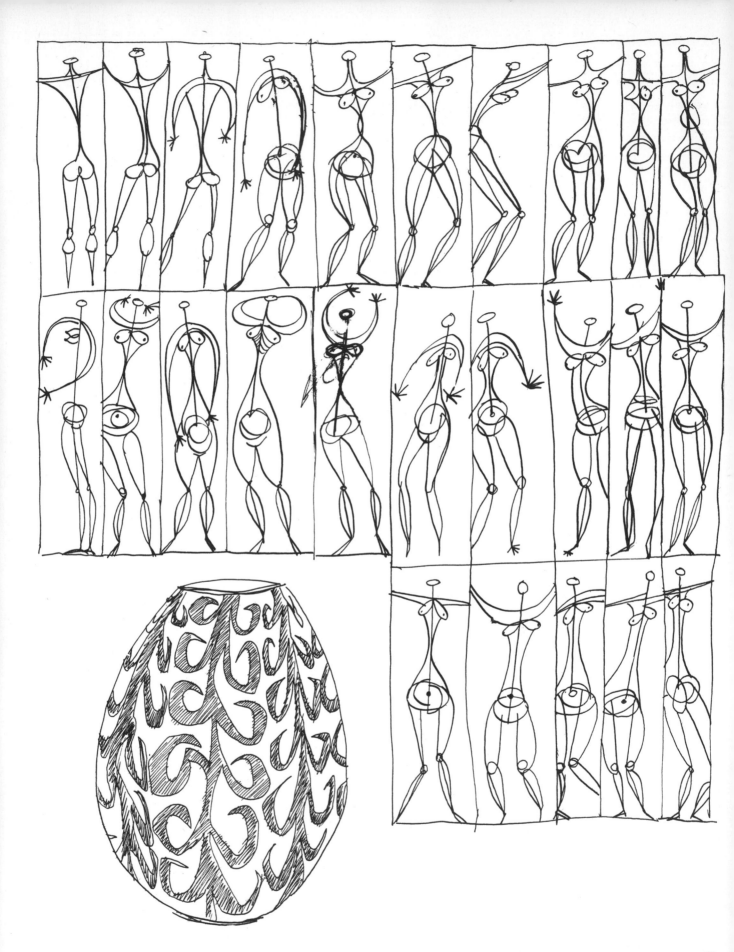

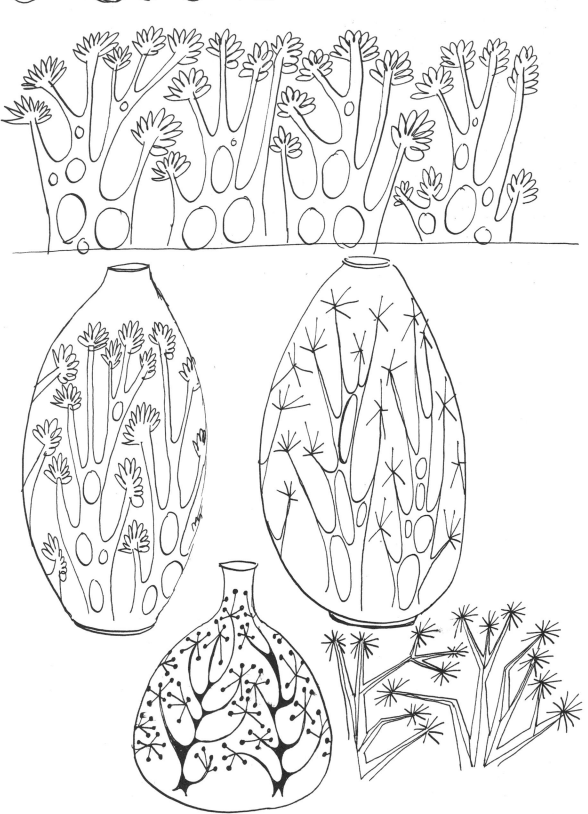

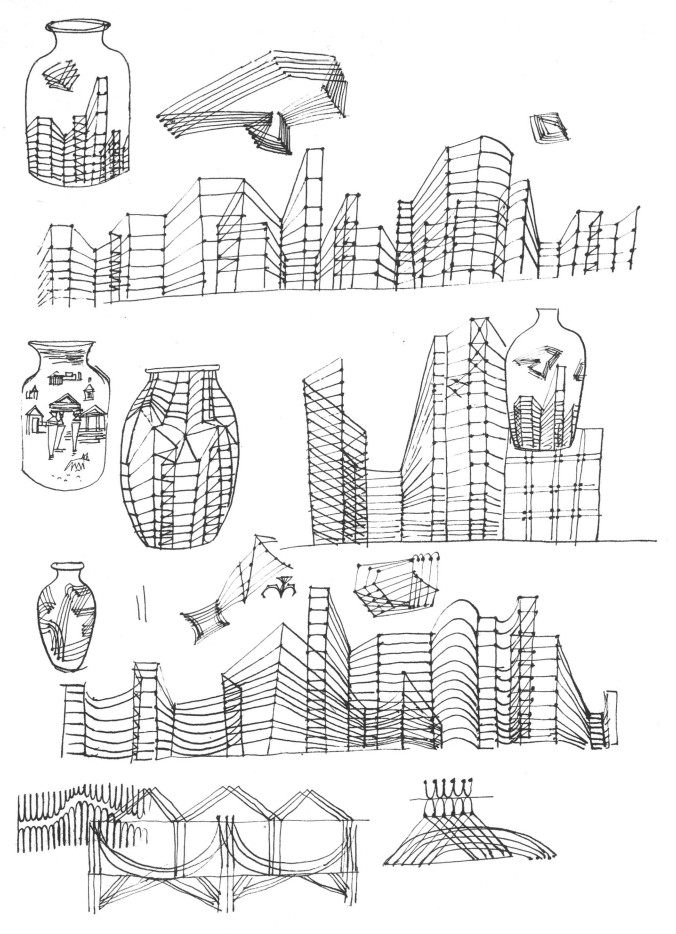

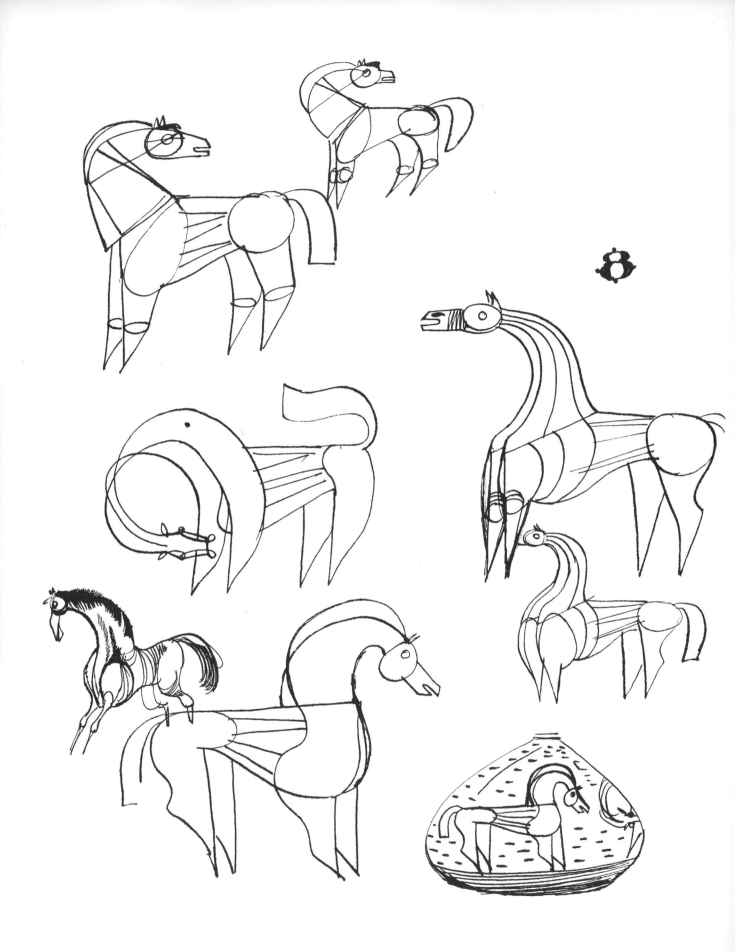

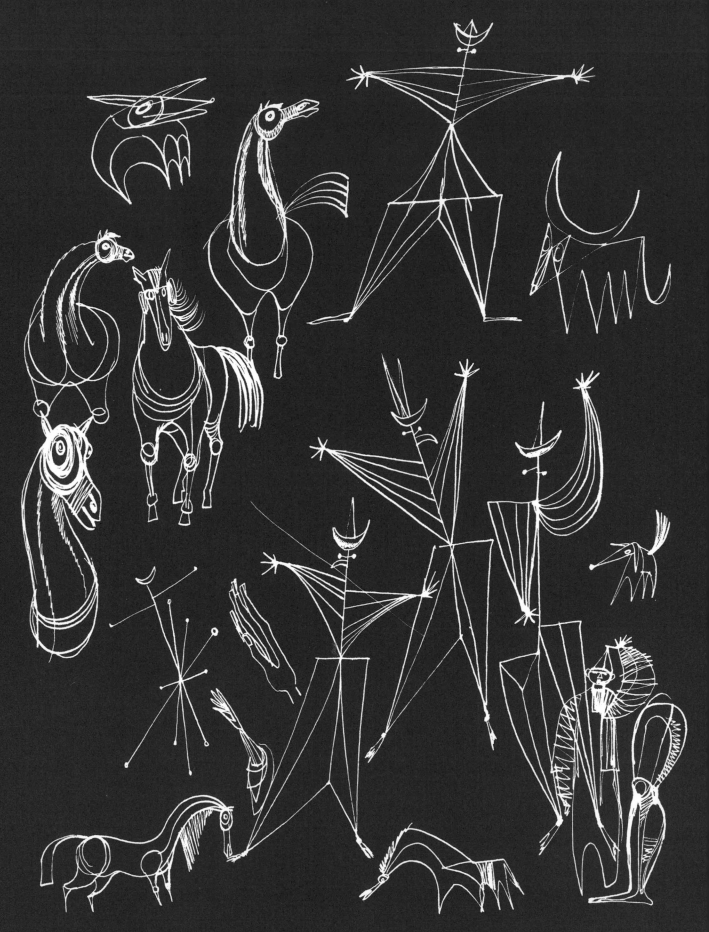

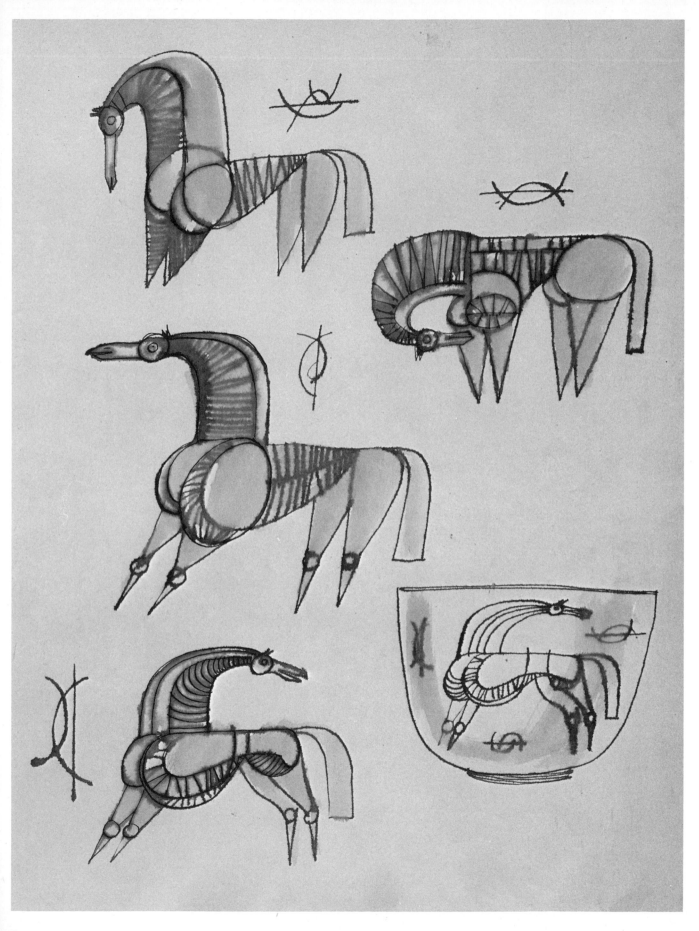

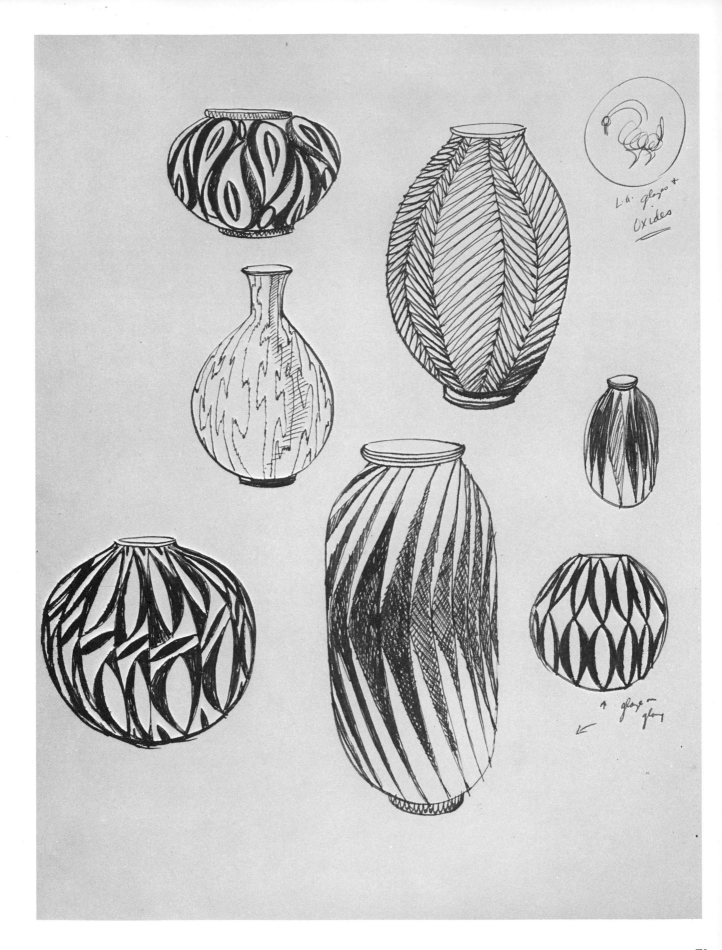

L.K. glaze +
Oxides

↑ glaze on
glaze

70

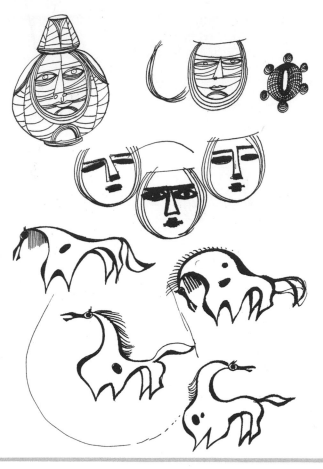

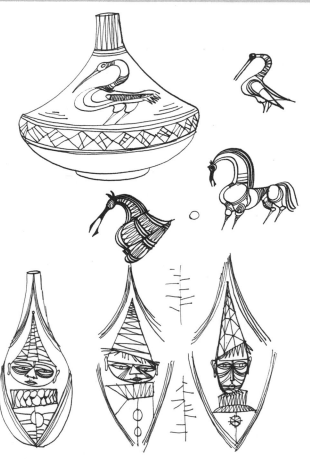

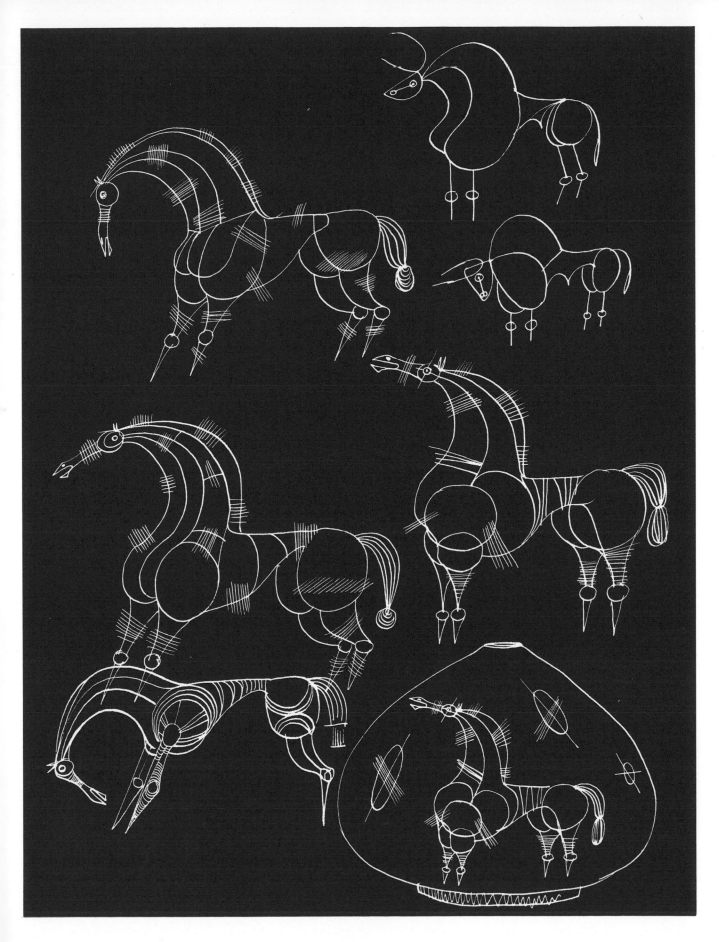

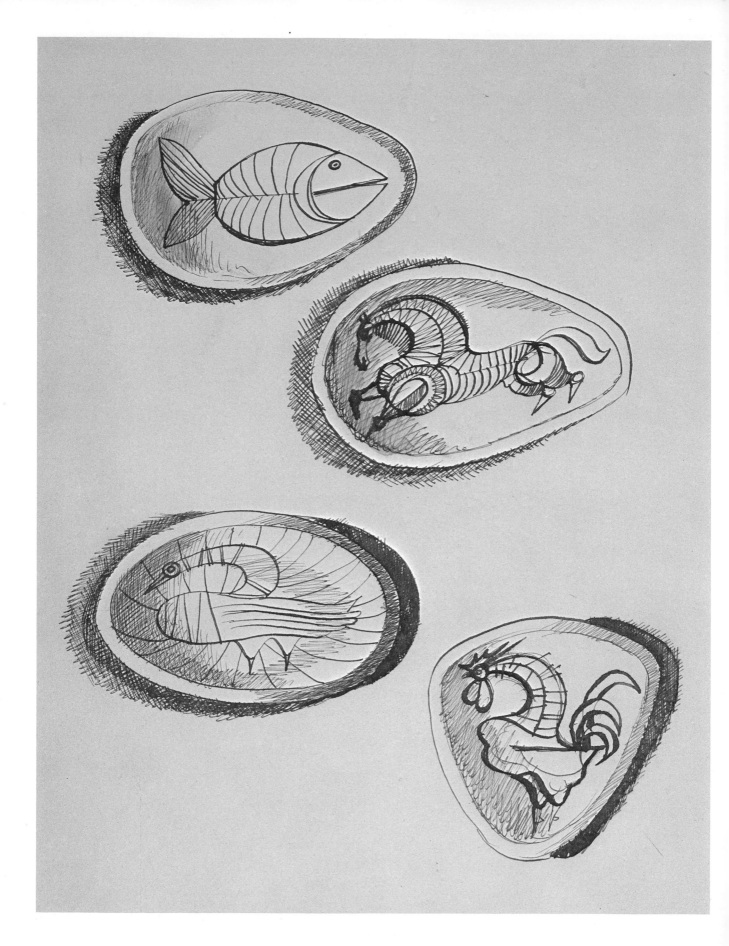

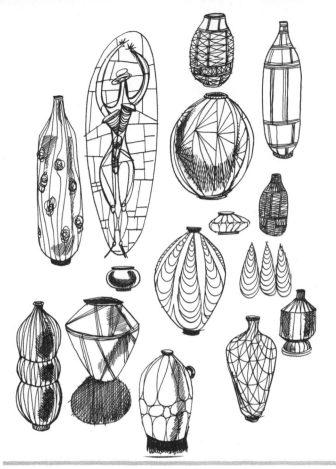

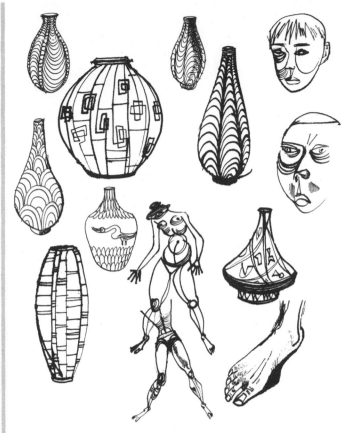

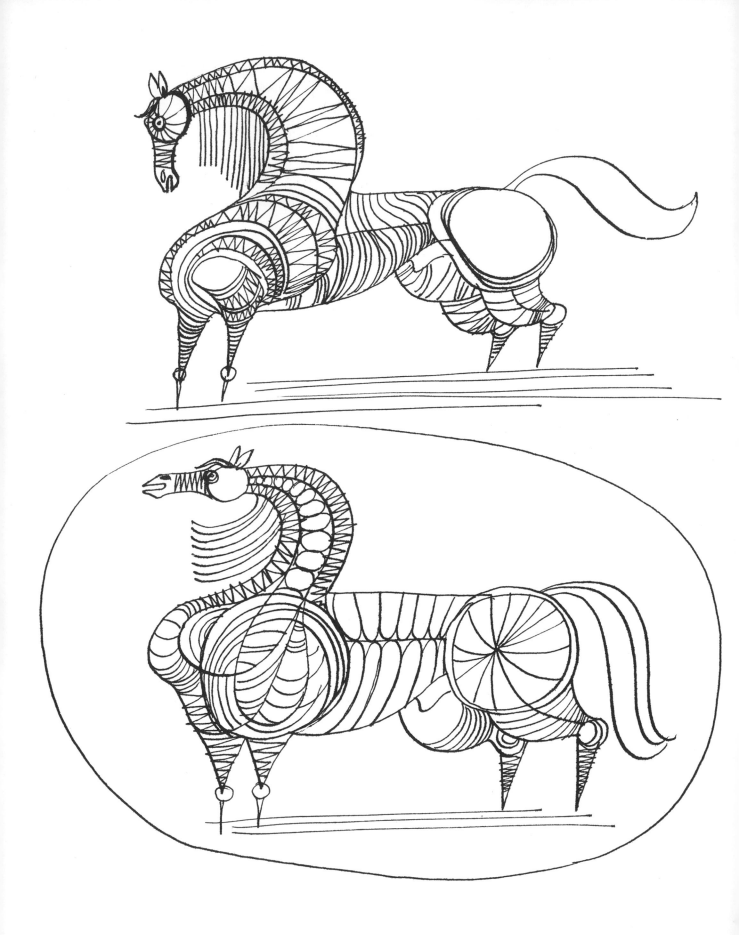

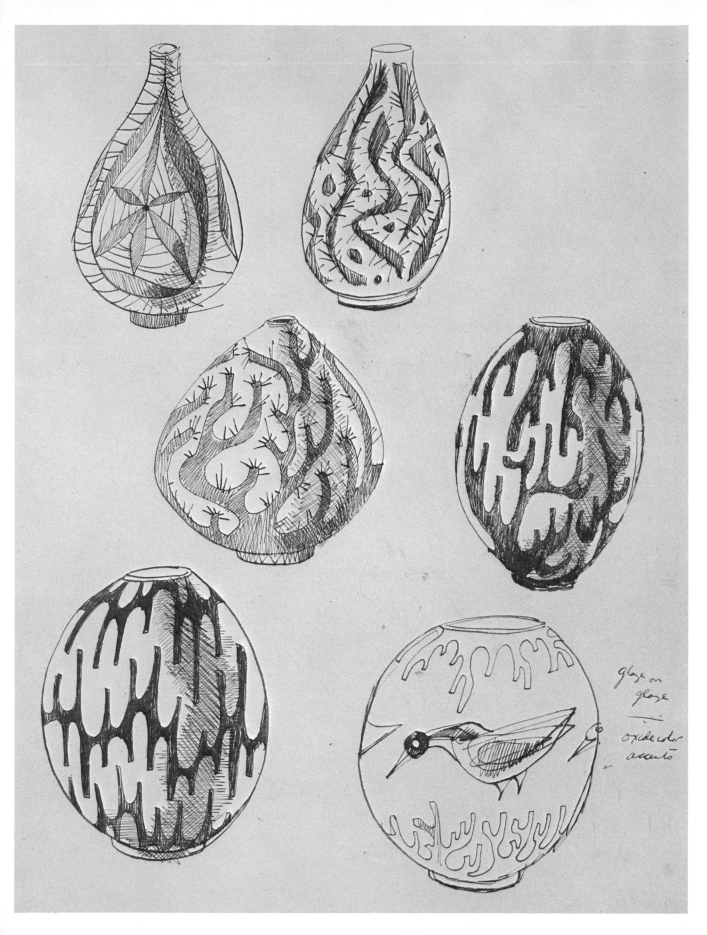

glaze on
glaze

oxide color
accents

79

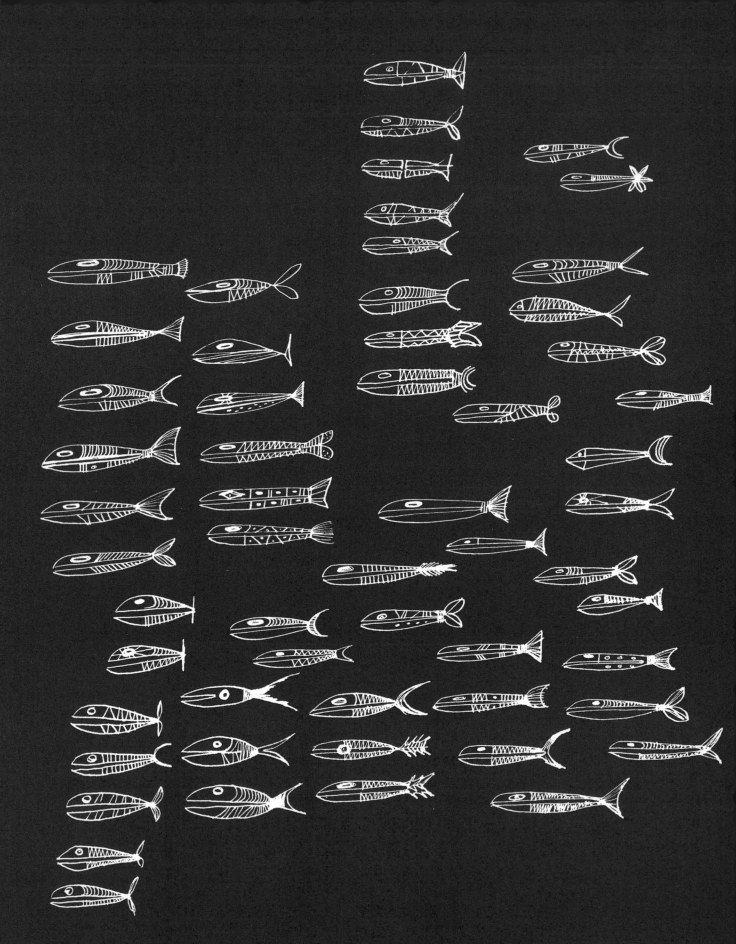

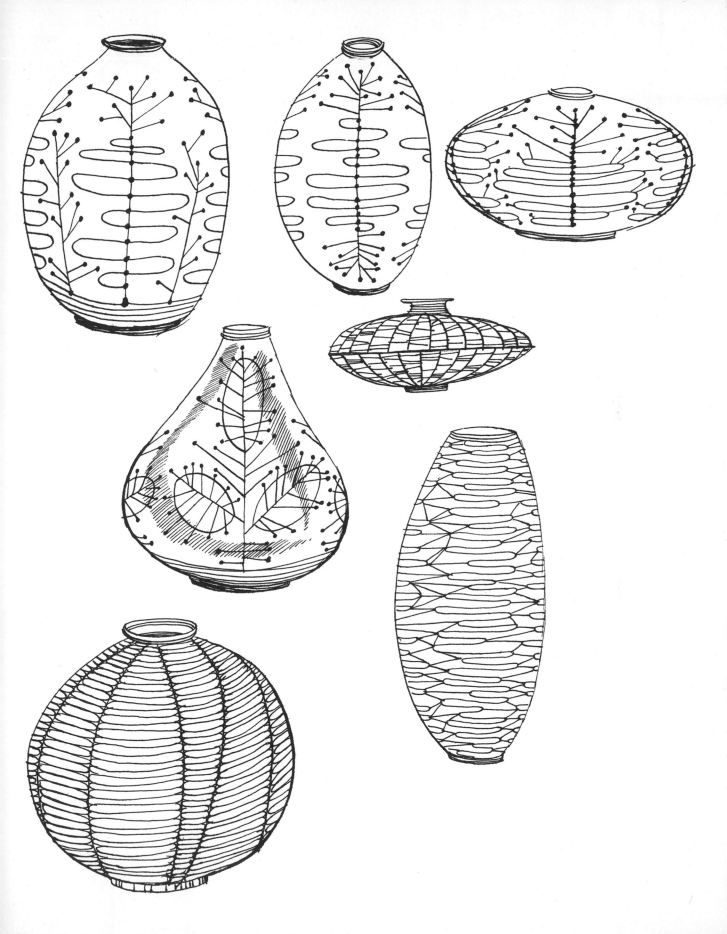

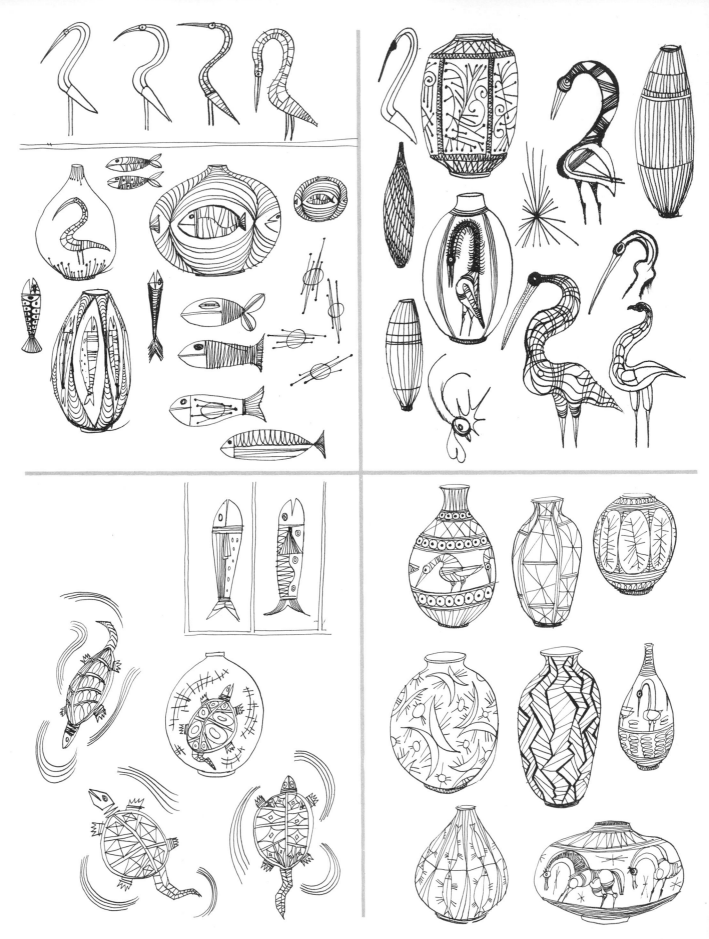

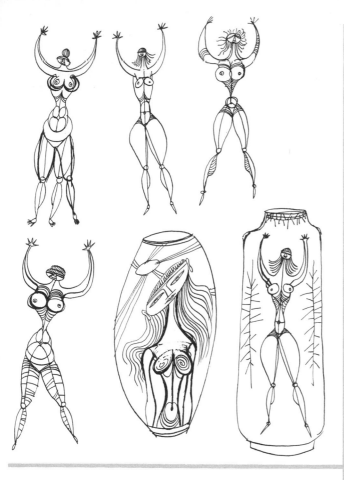

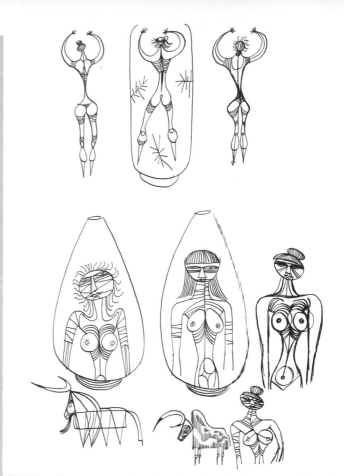

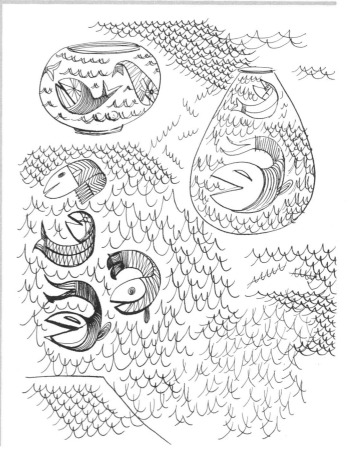

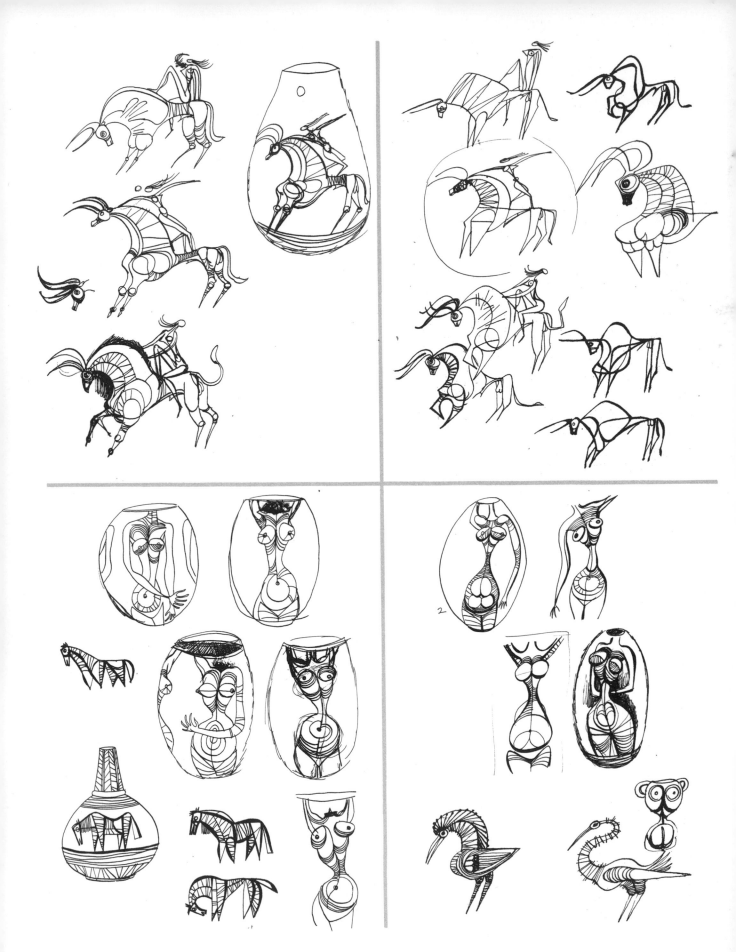

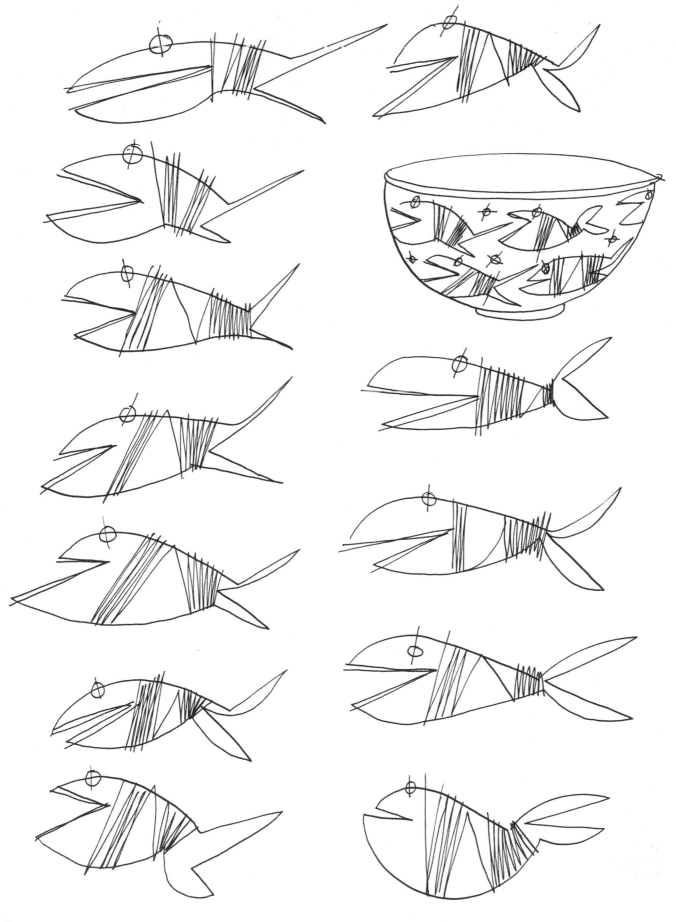

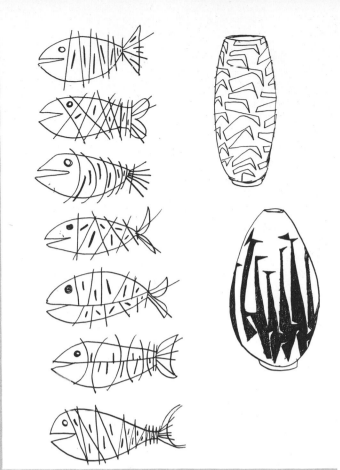

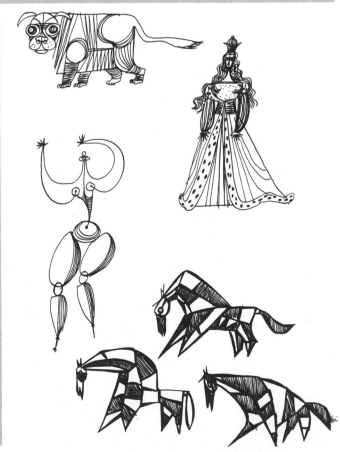

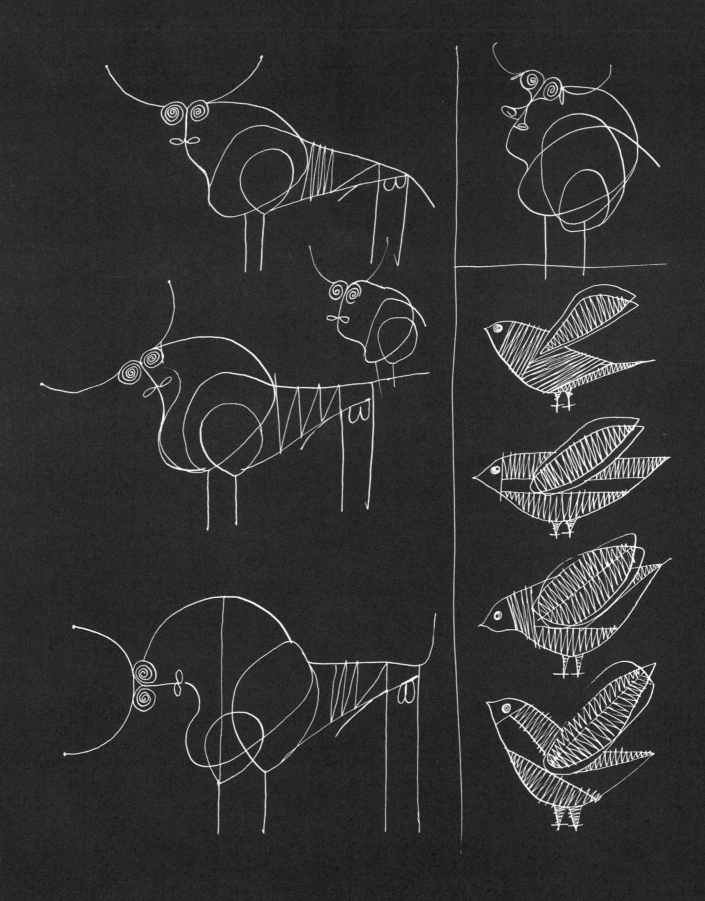

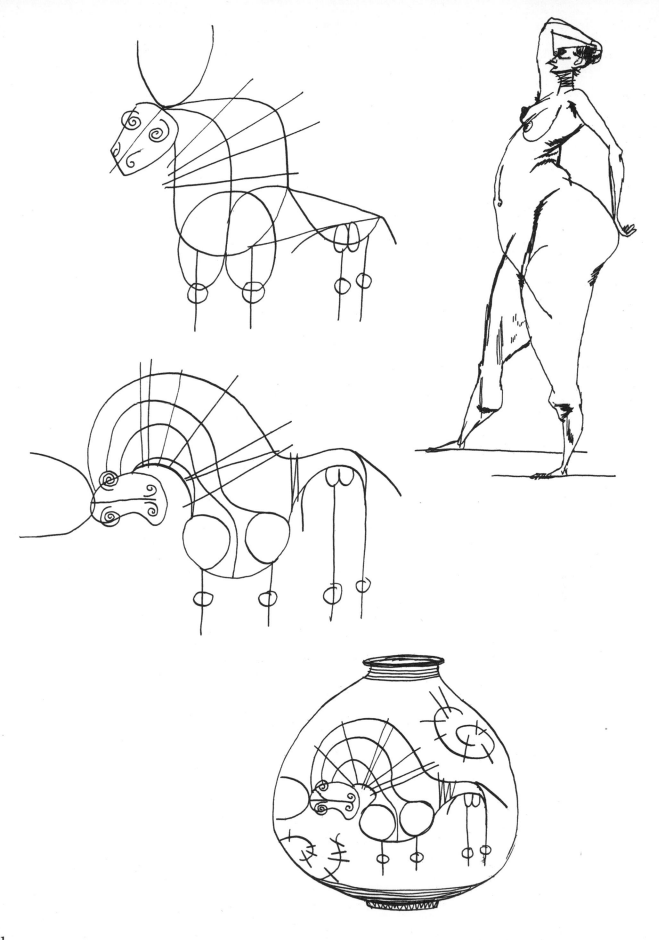

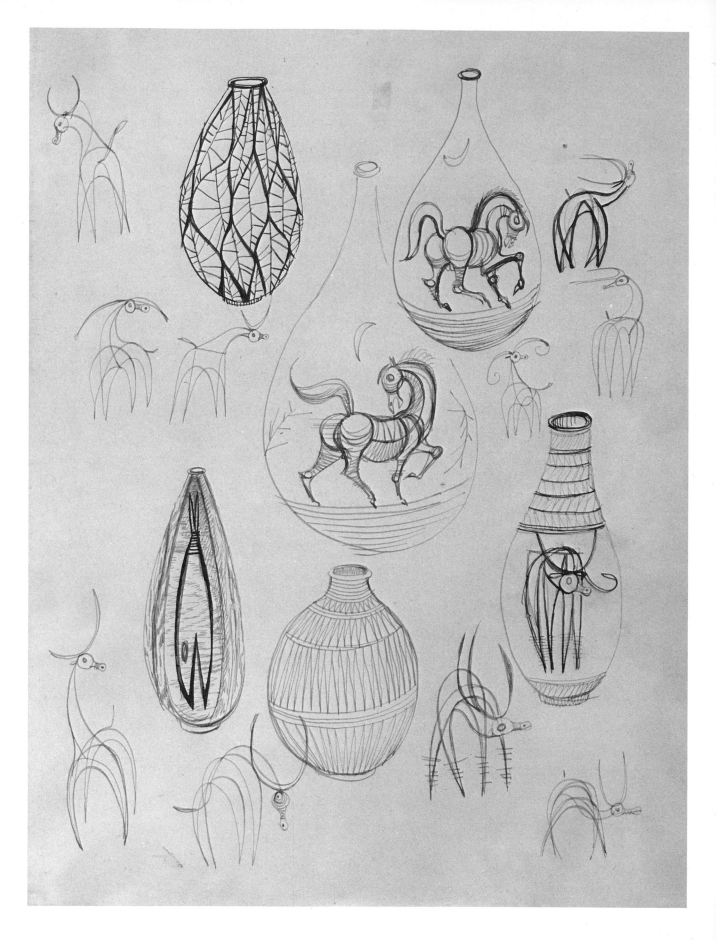

93

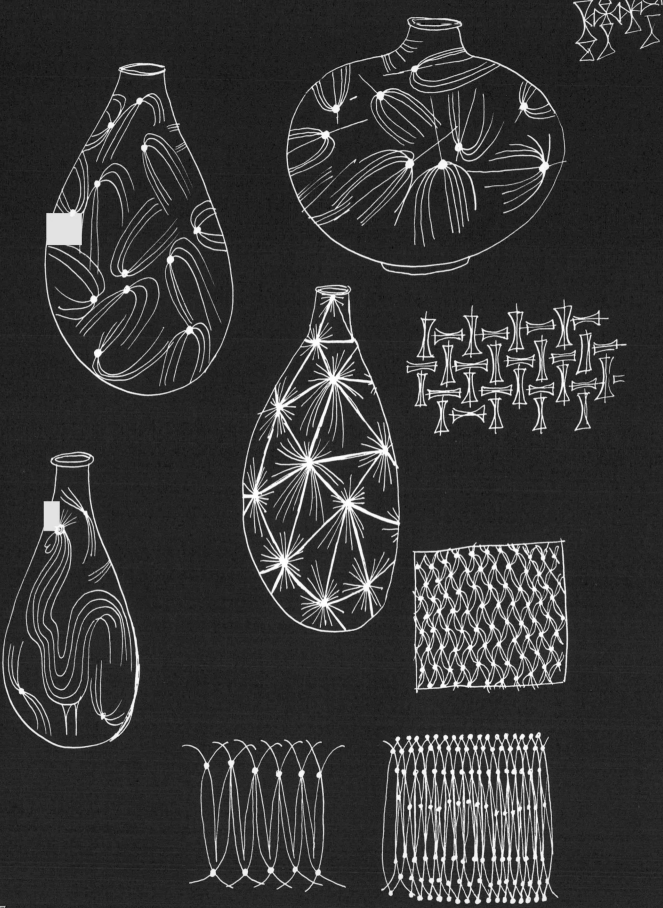

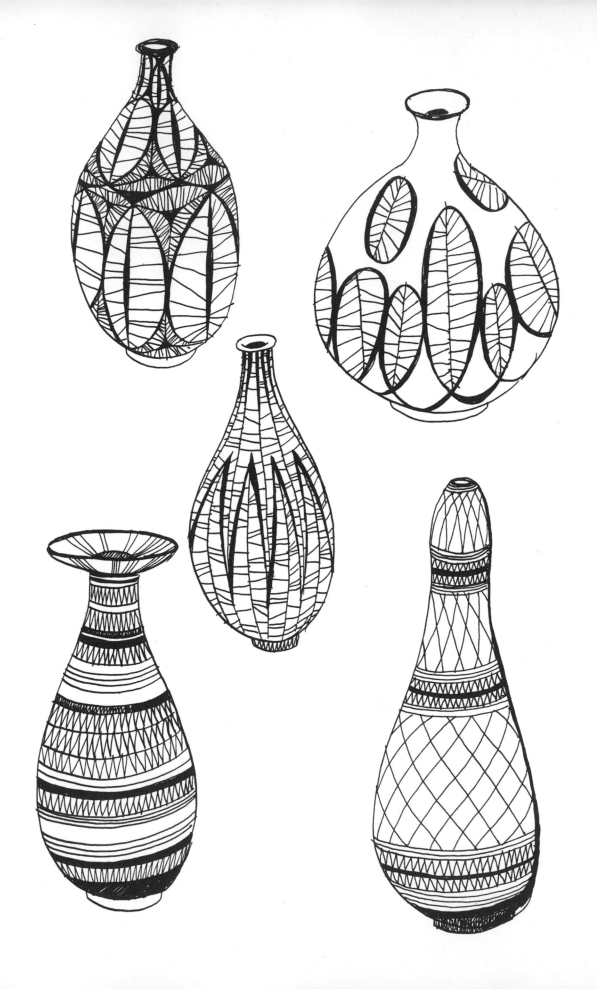

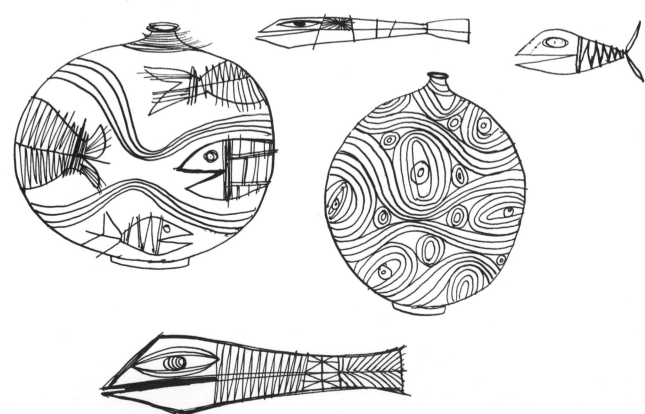

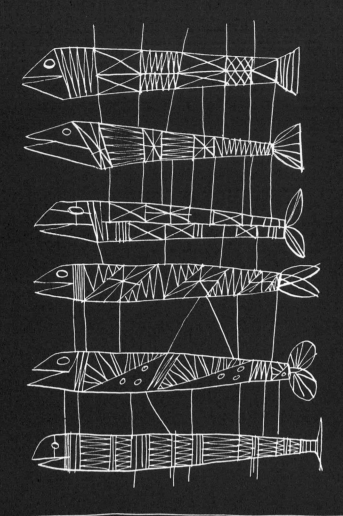

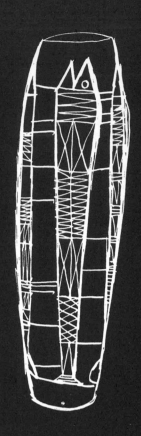

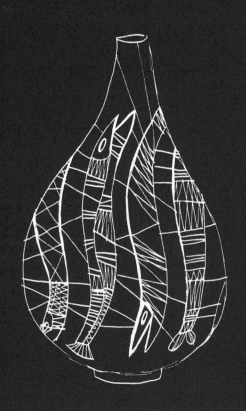

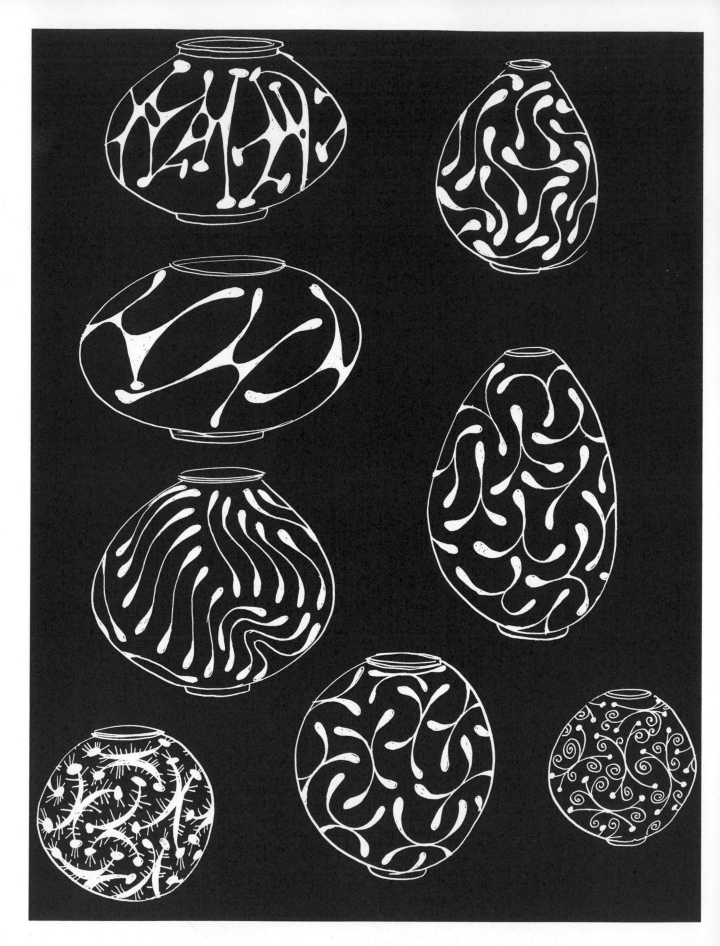

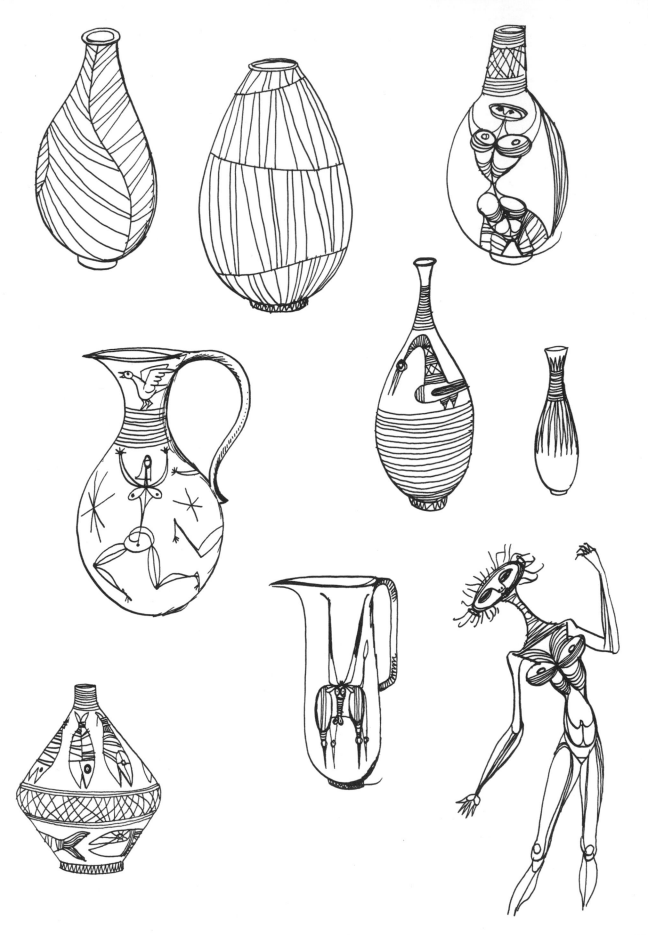

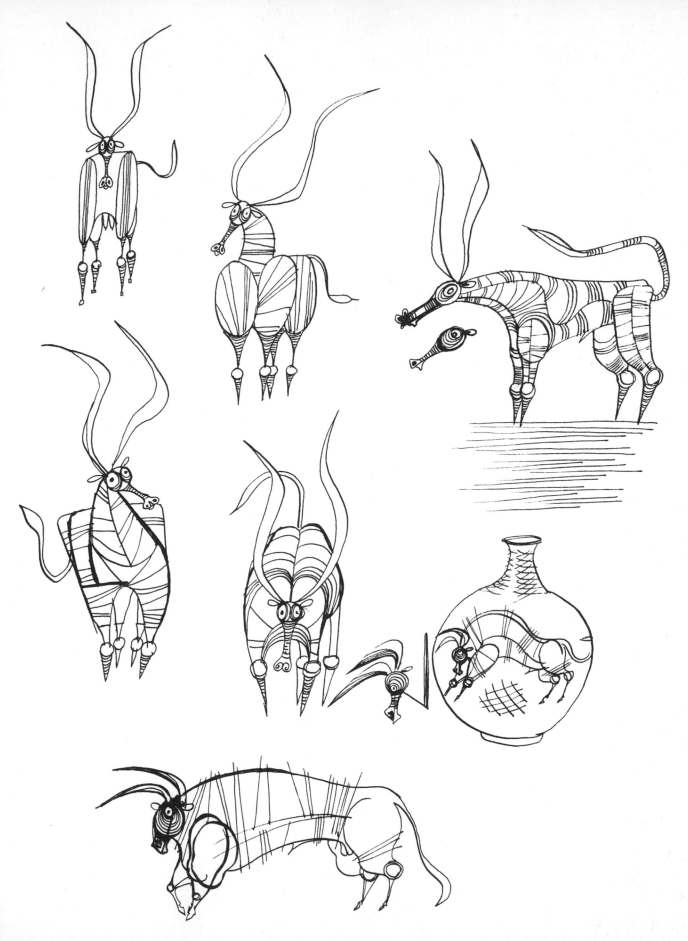

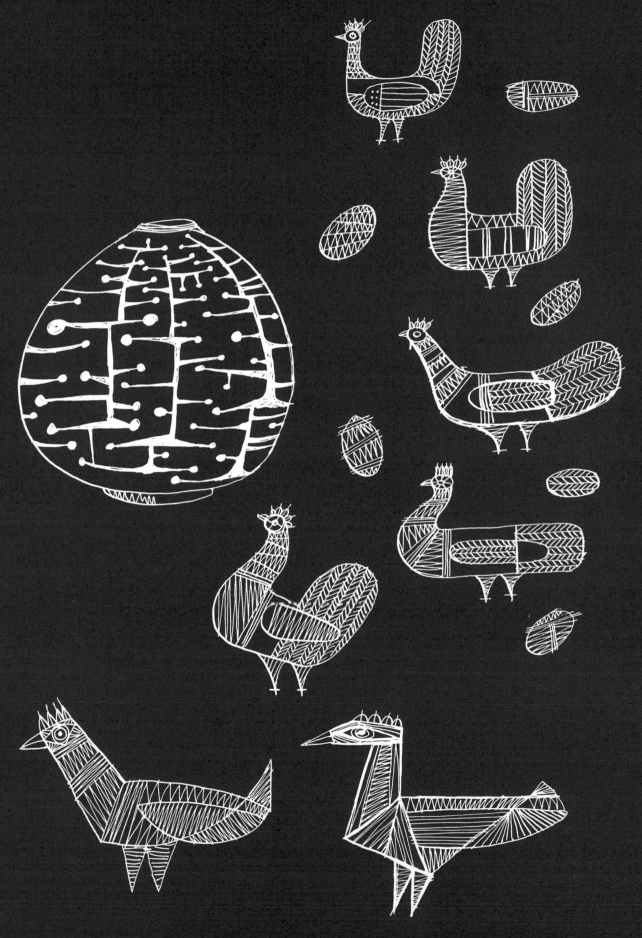

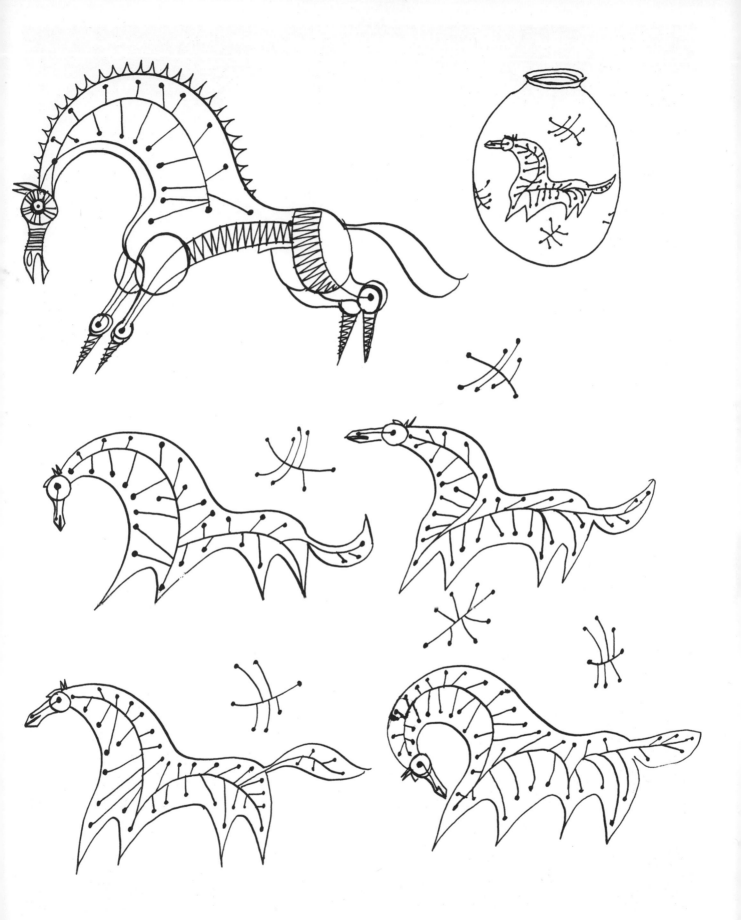

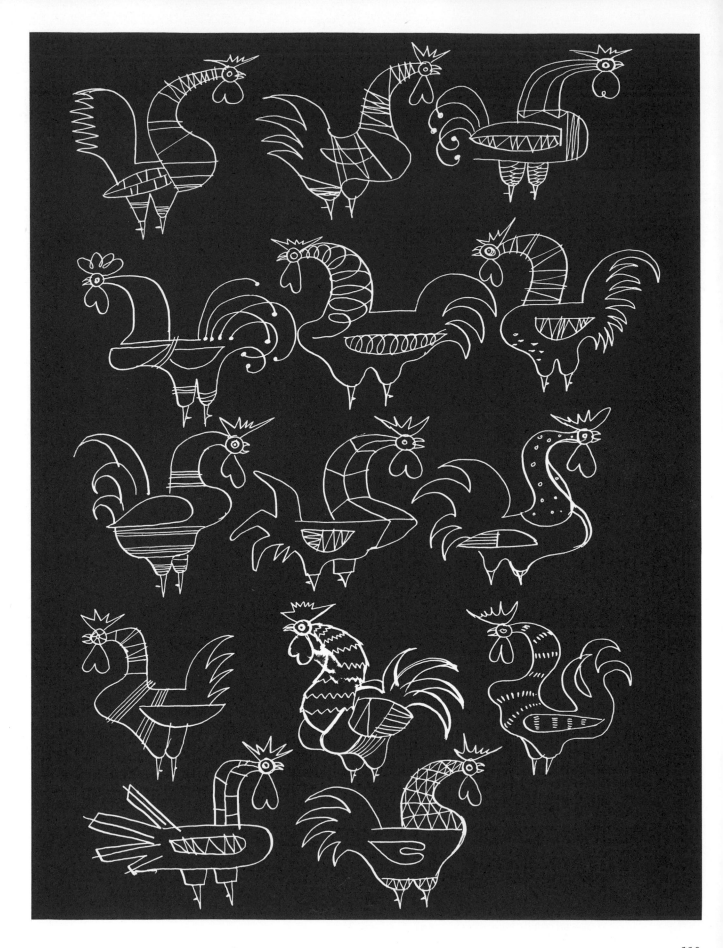

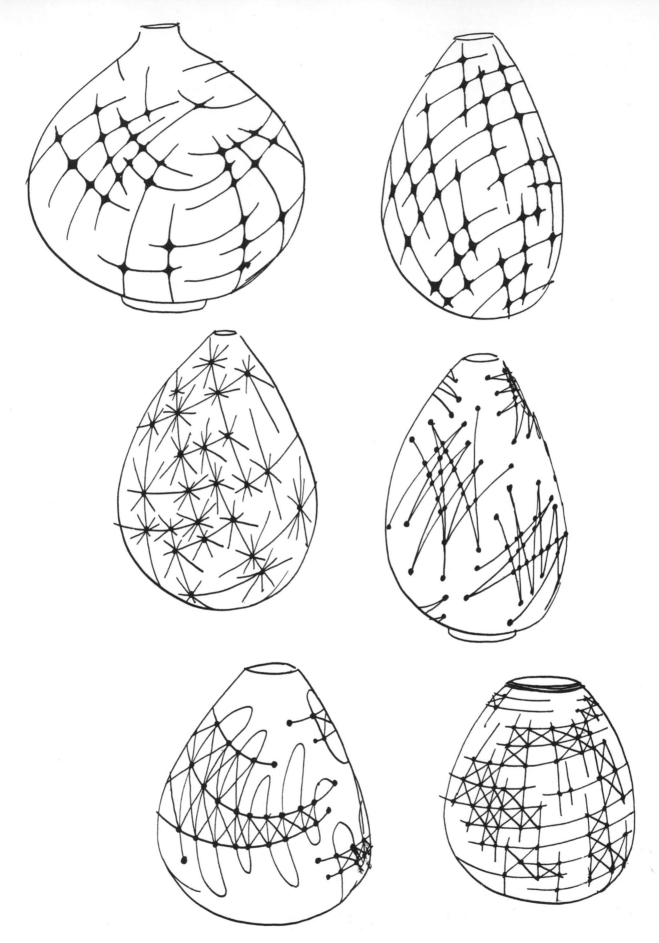

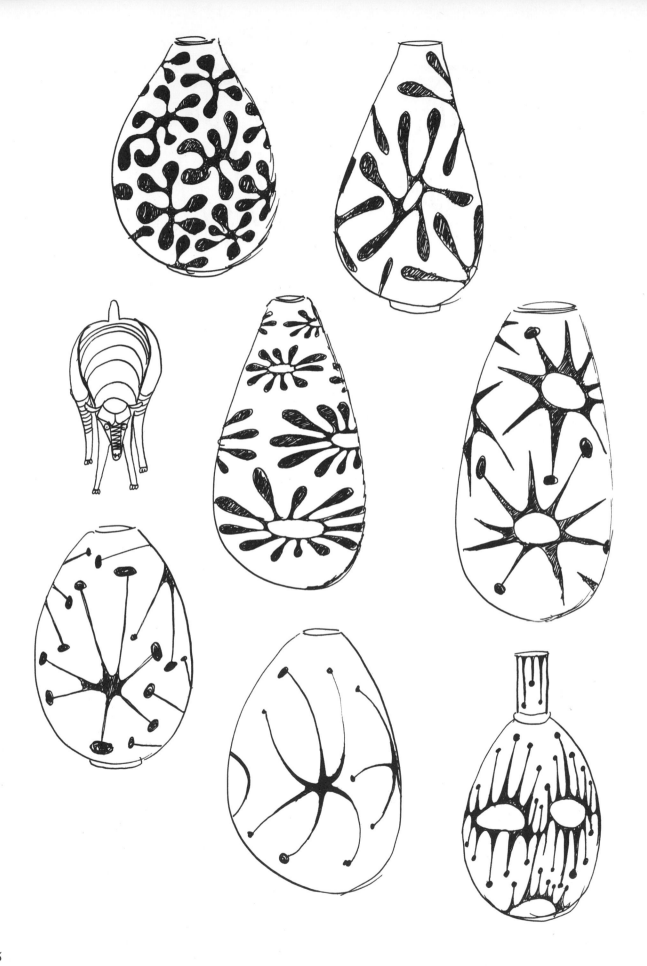

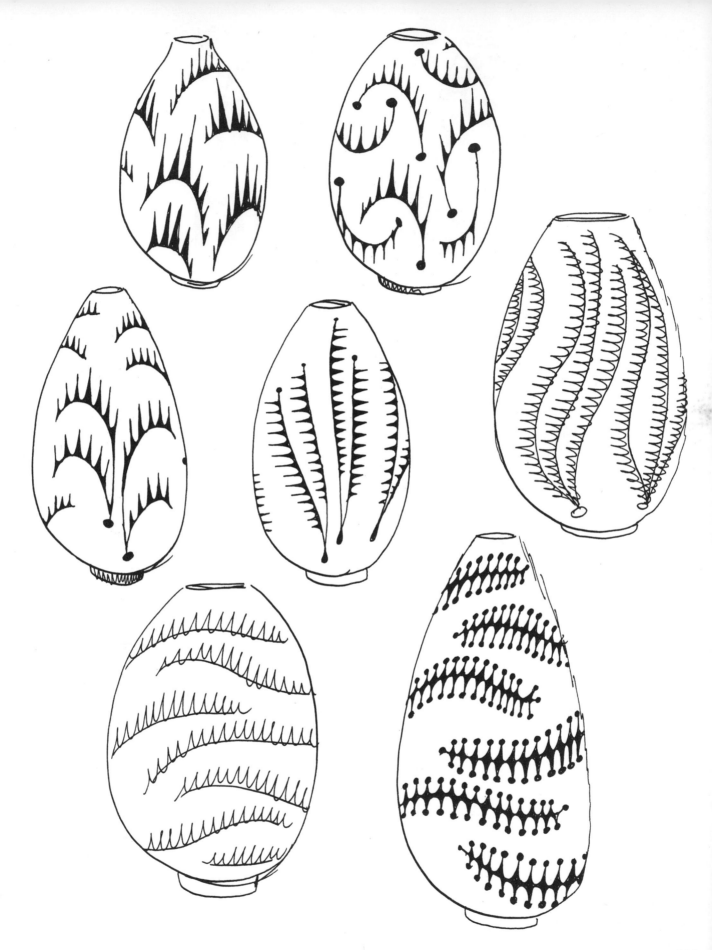

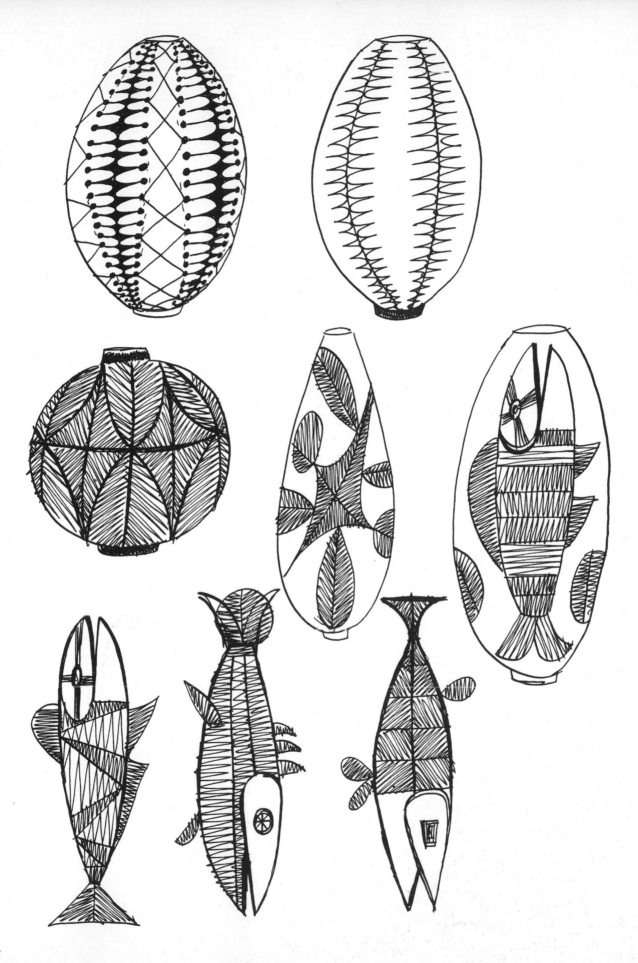

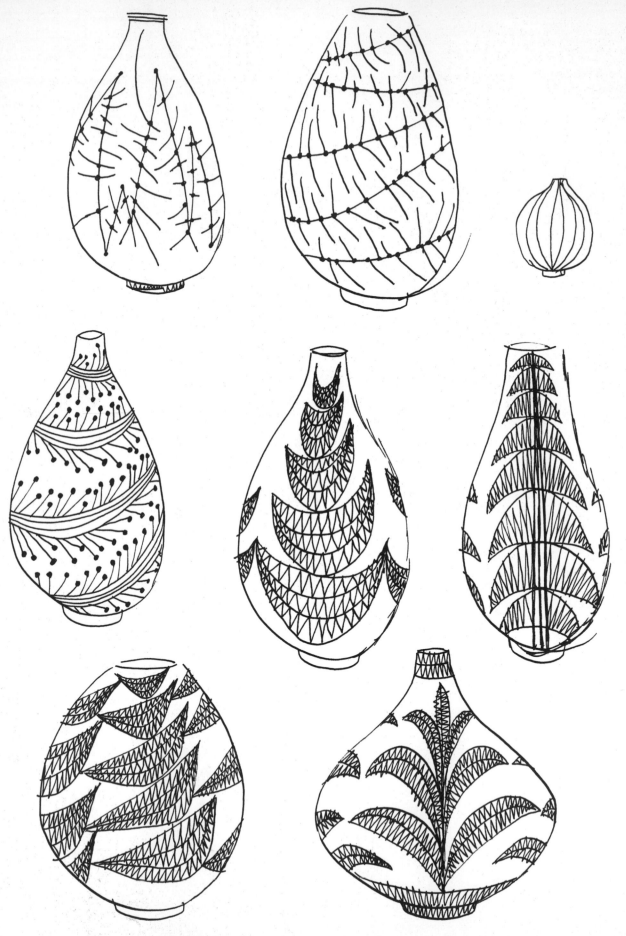

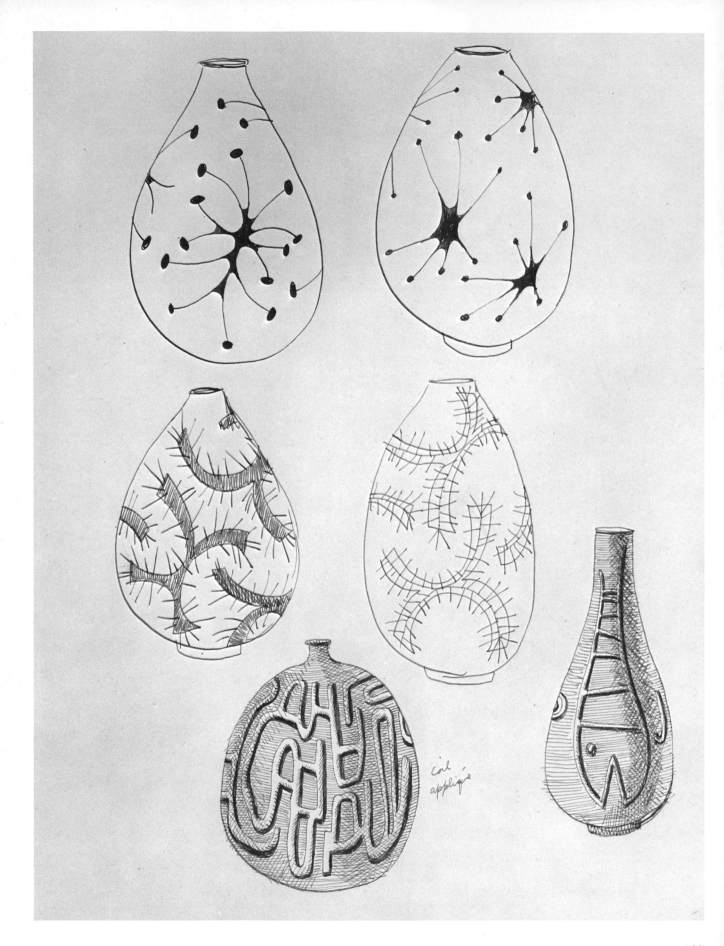

coil
appliqué

122

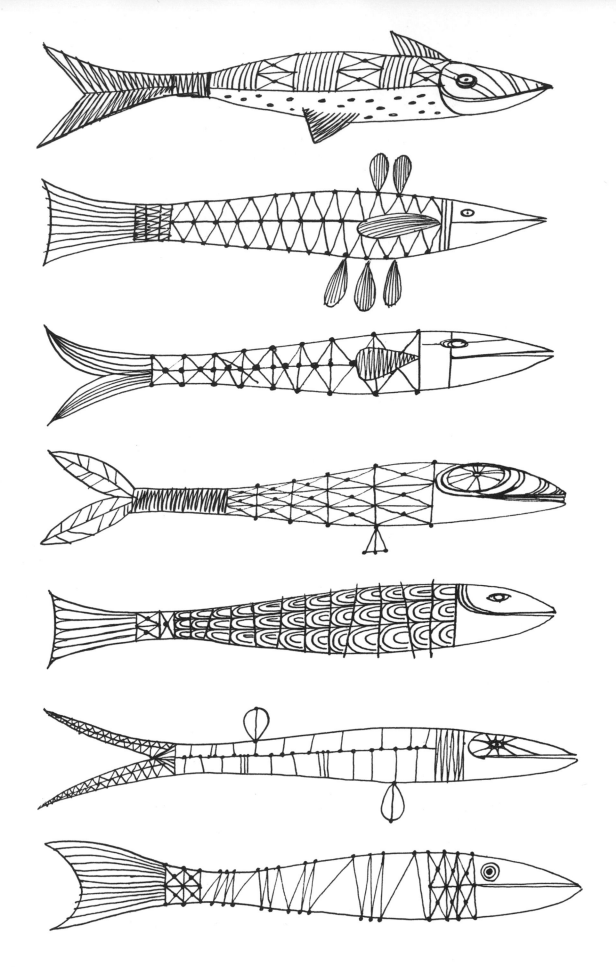

124

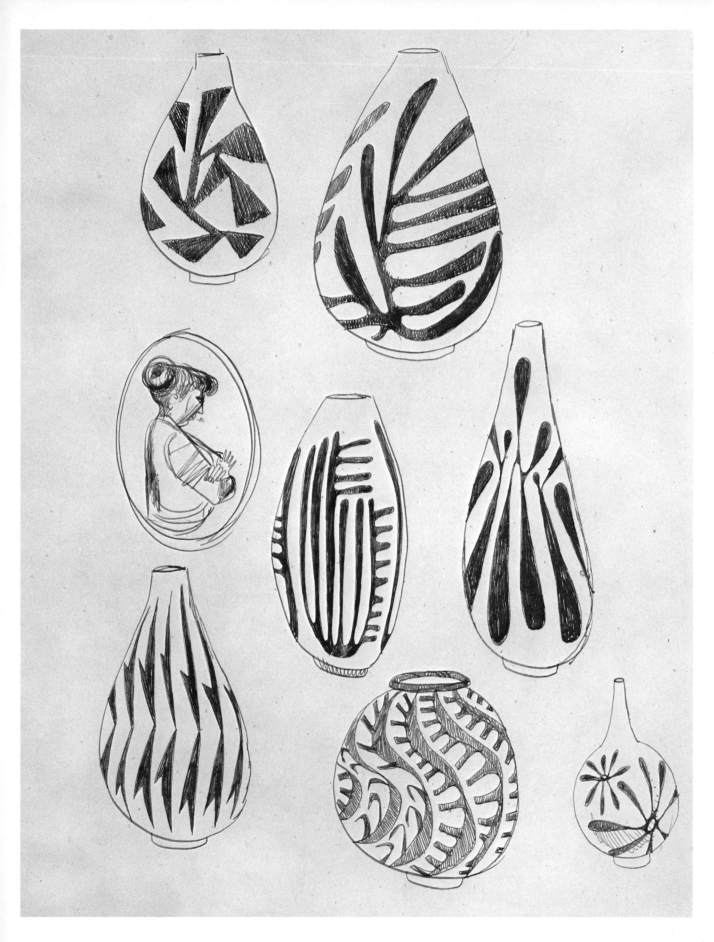

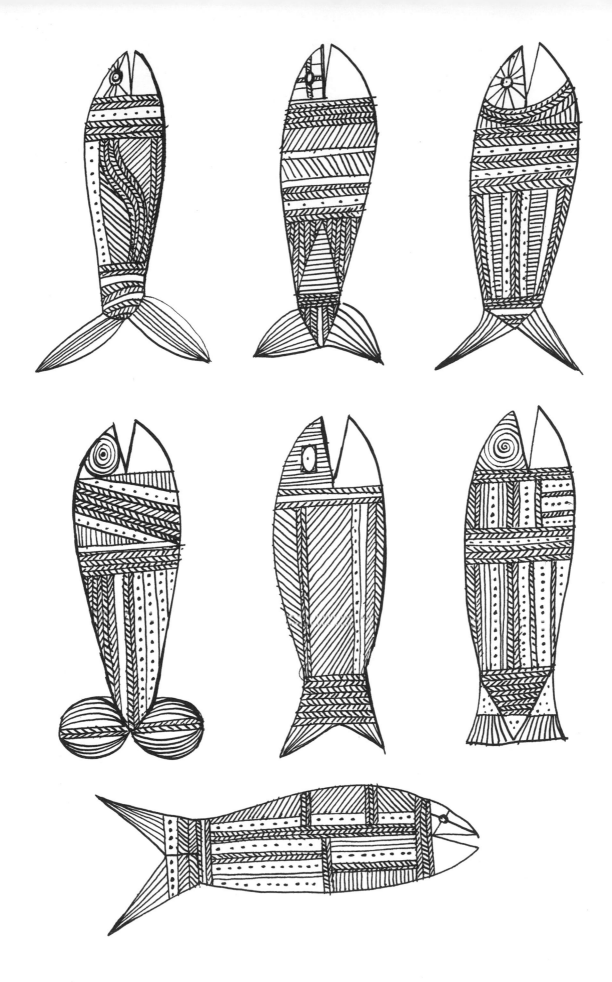

129

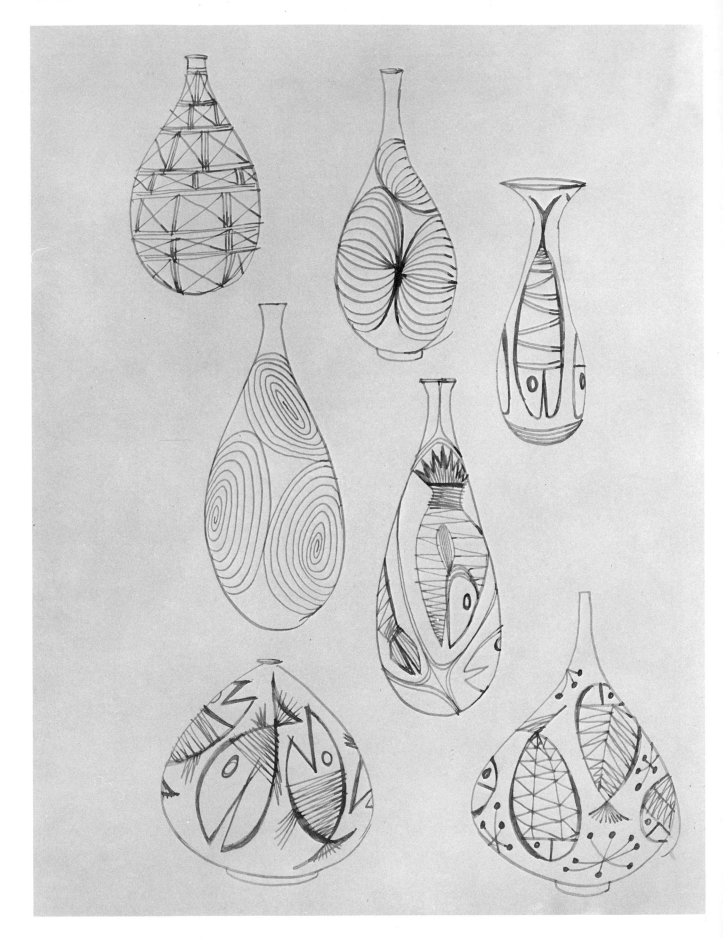

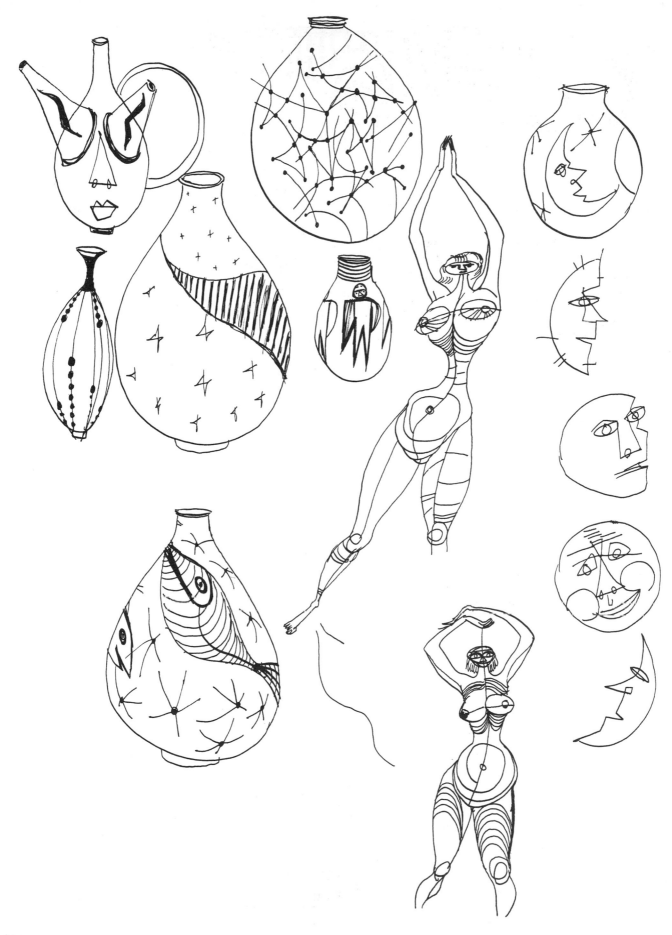

131

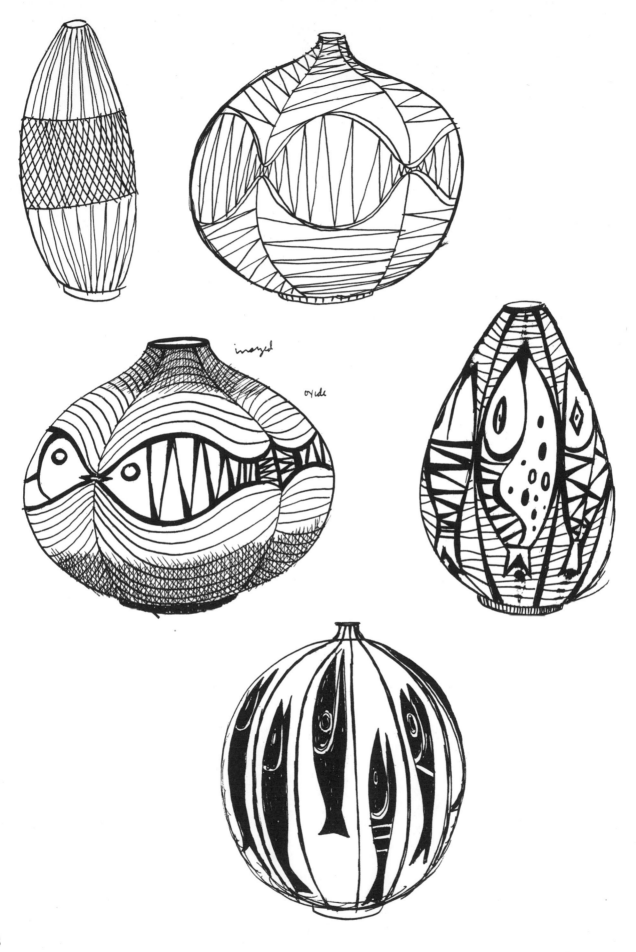

inoxyd

oxide

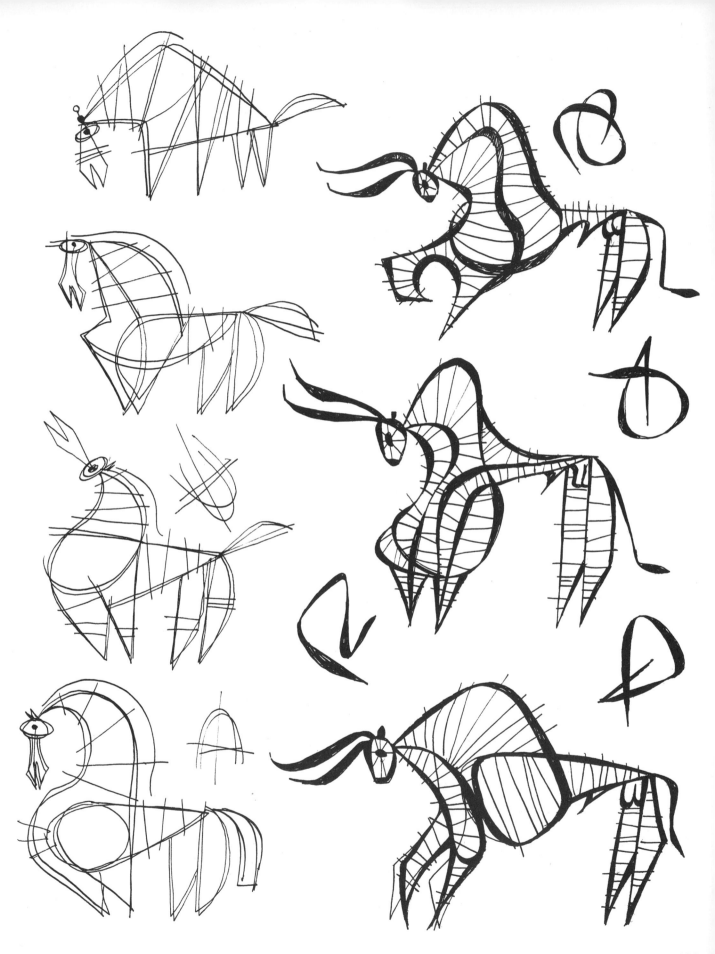

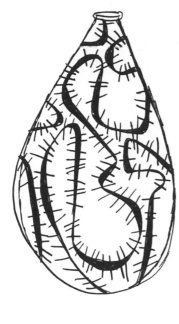

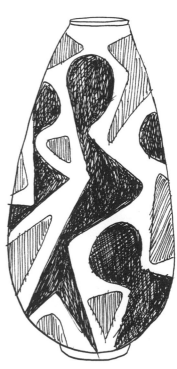

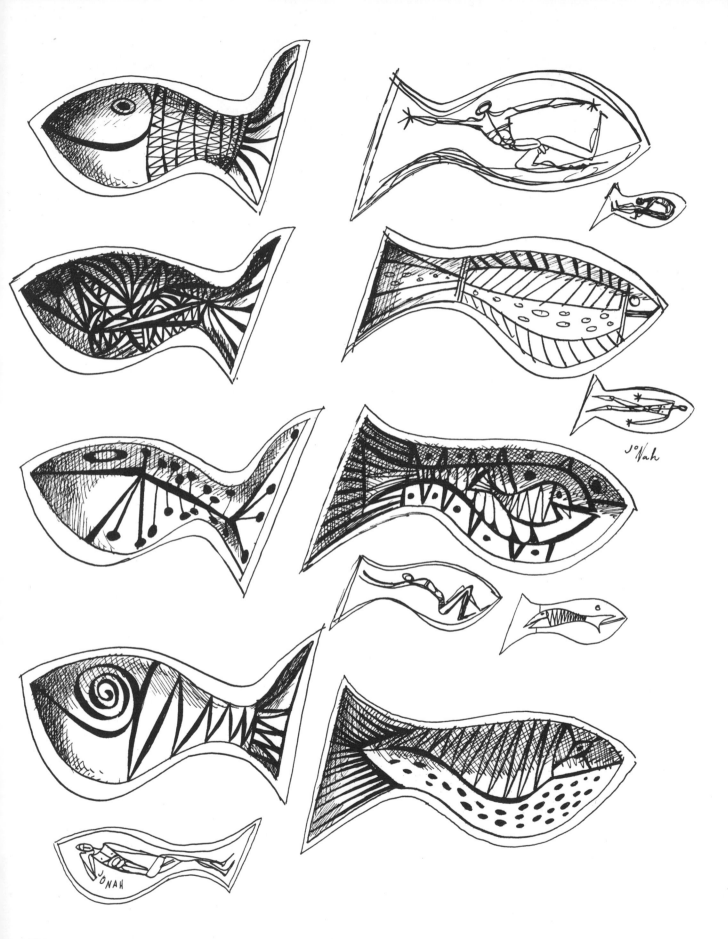

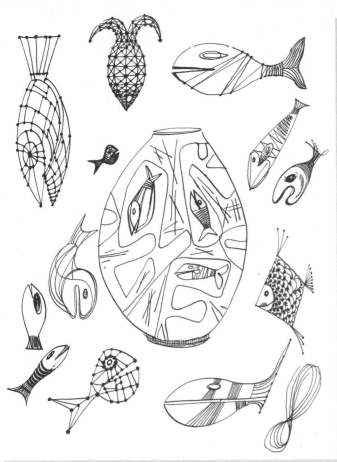
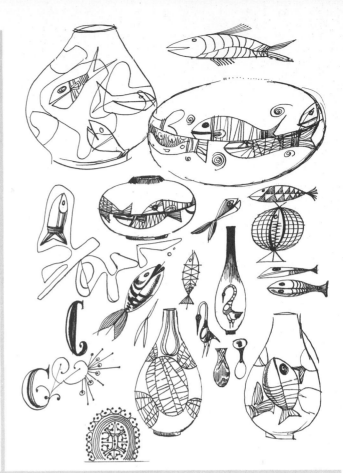
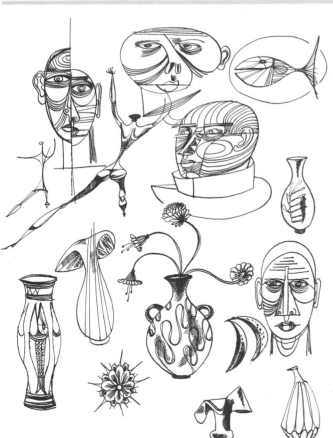
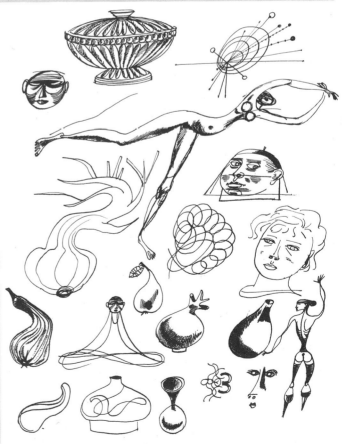

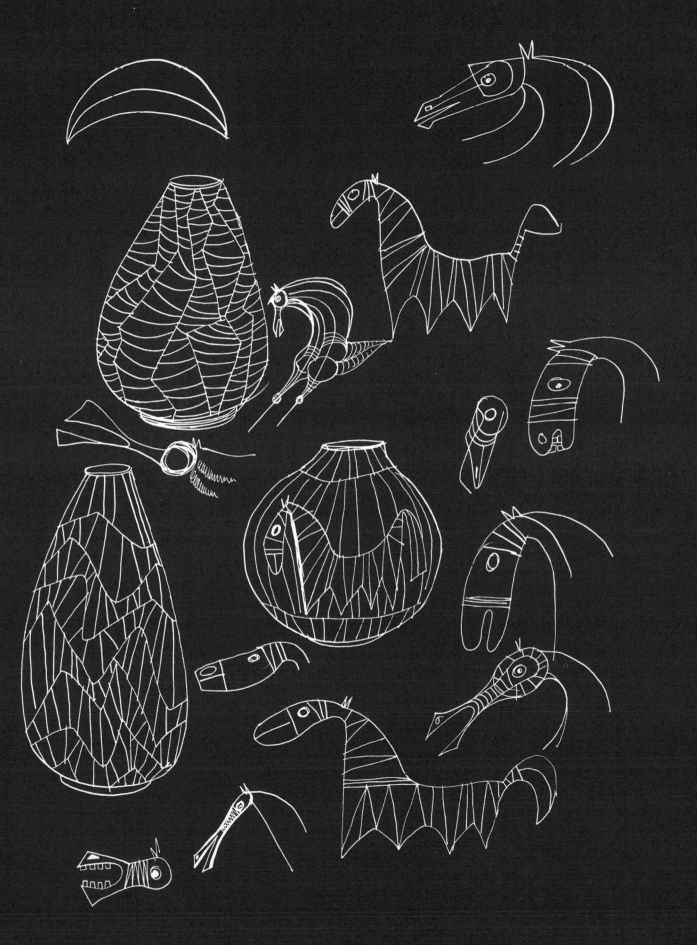

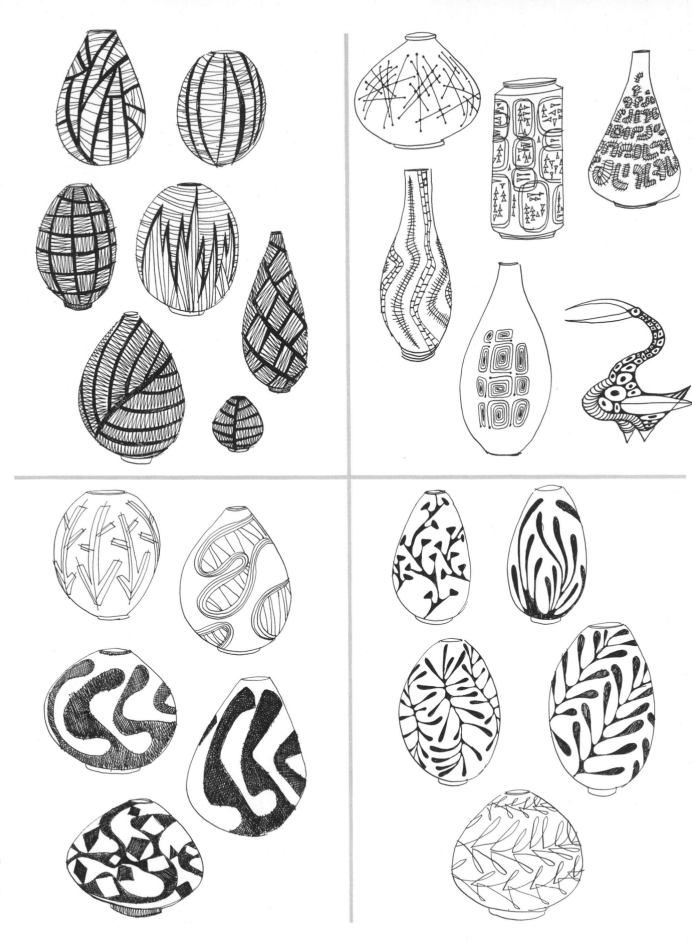

142

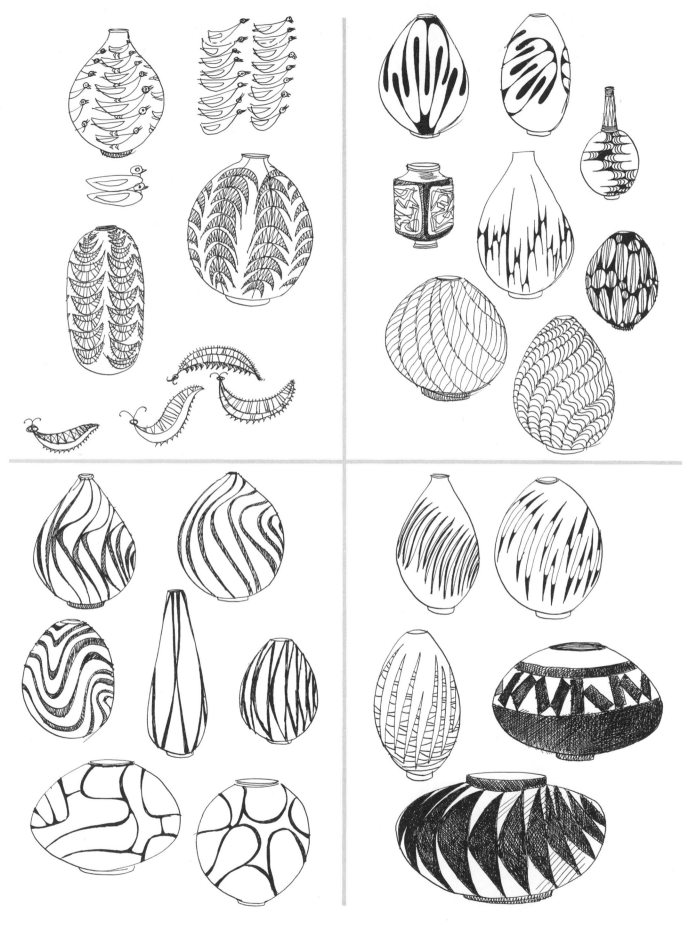

143

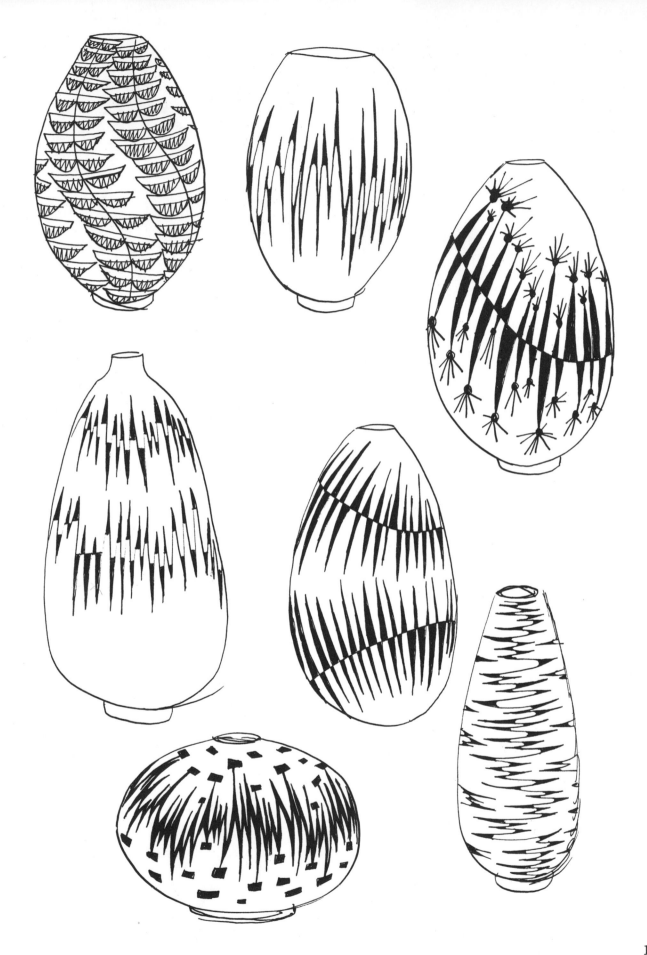

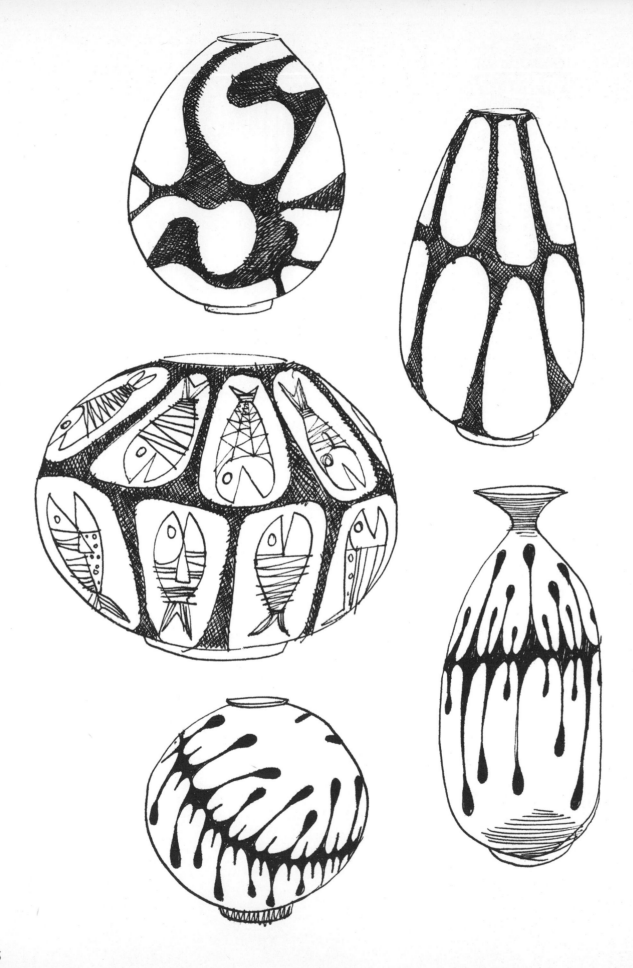

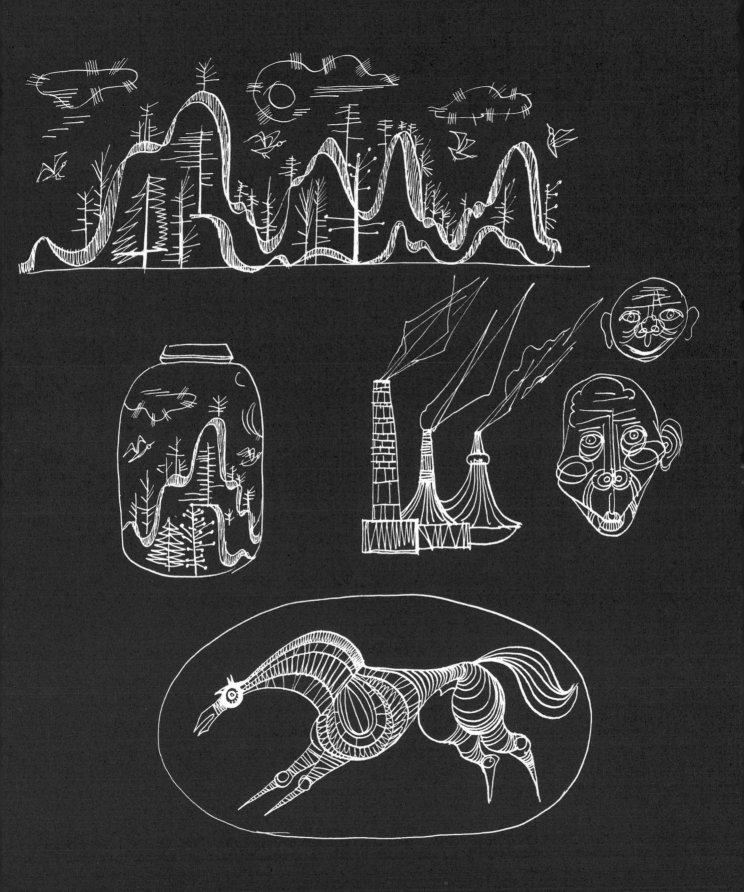

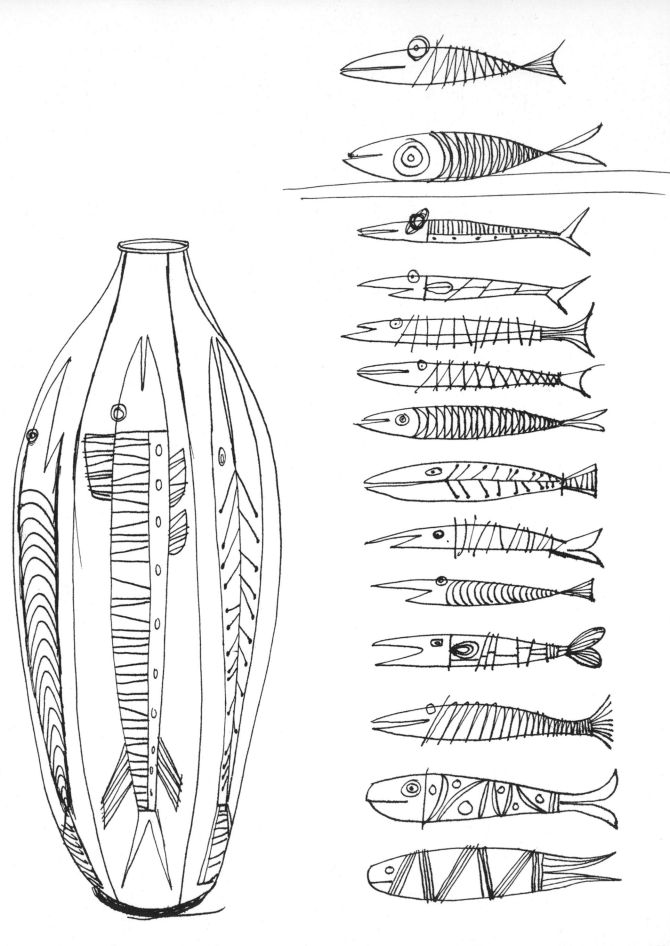

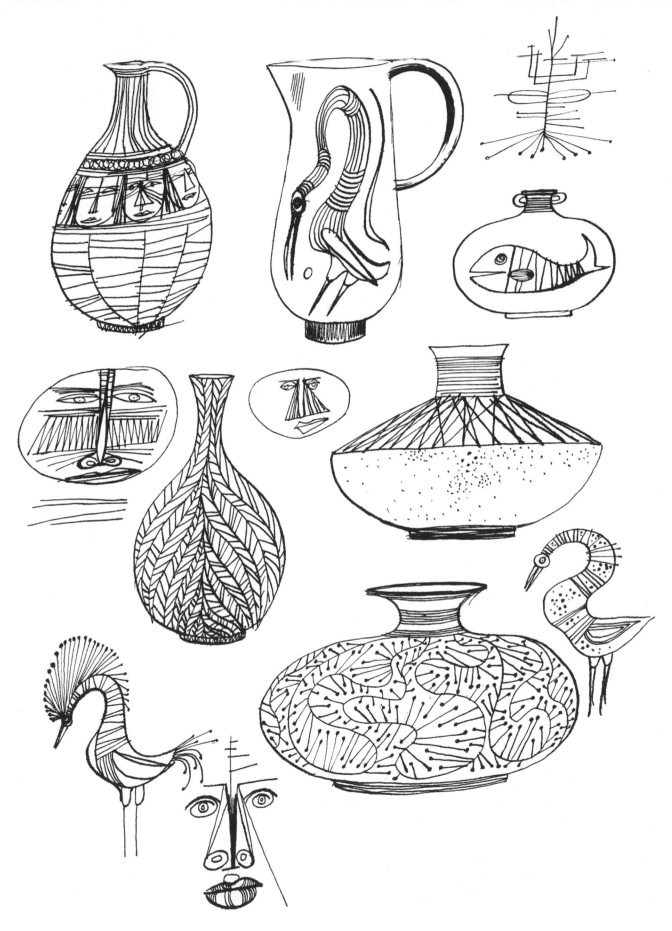

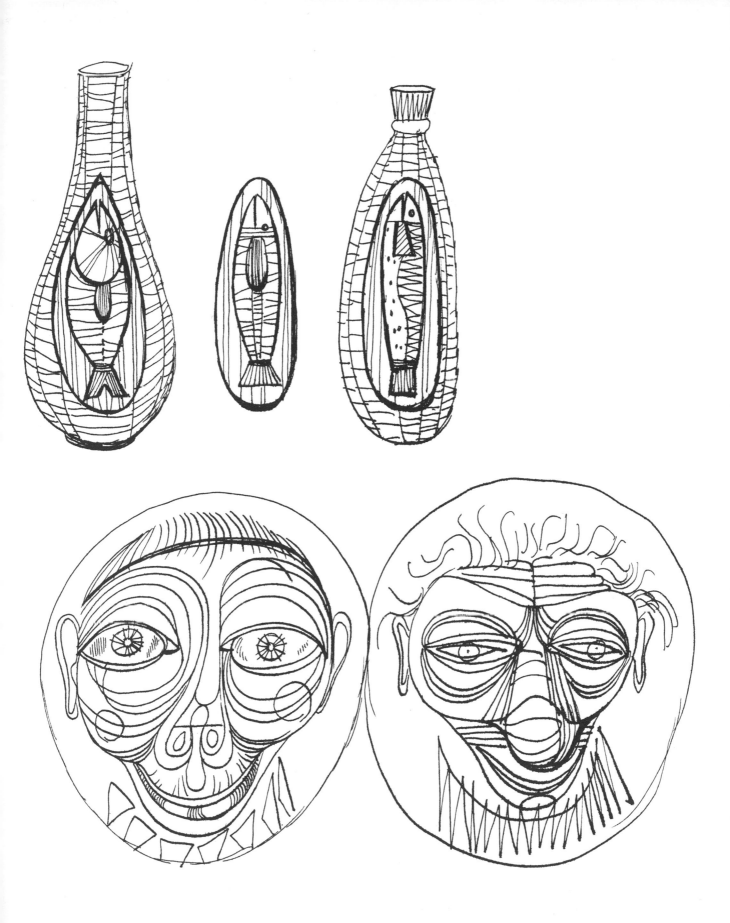

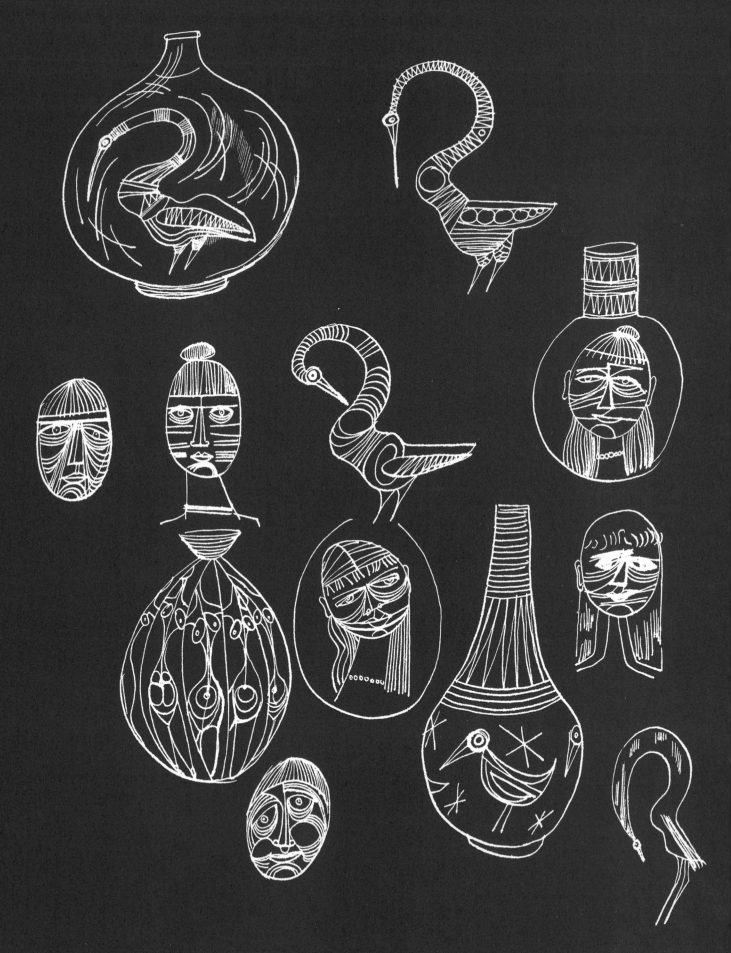

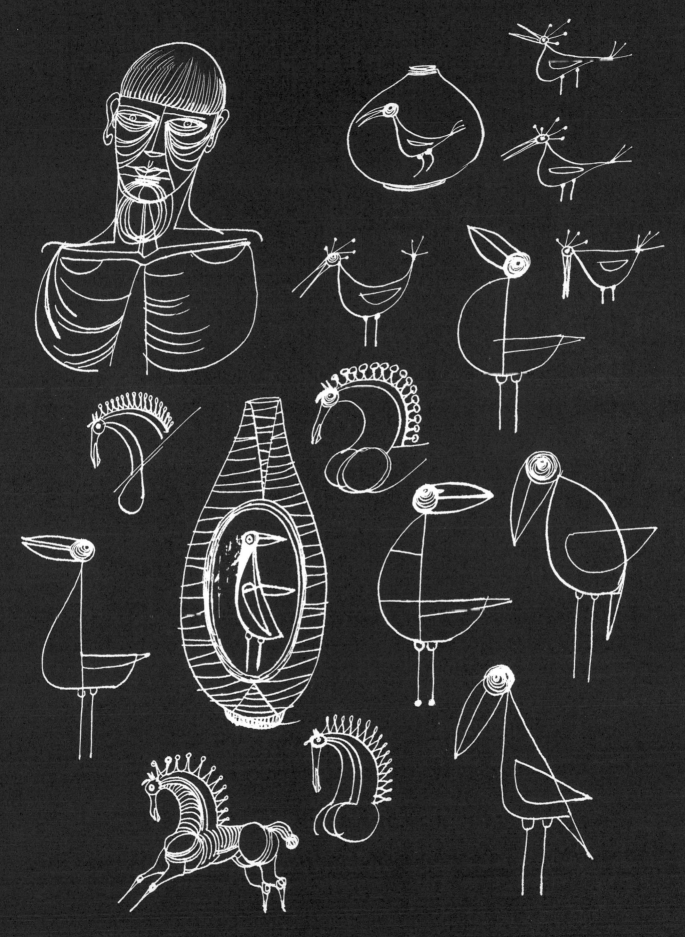

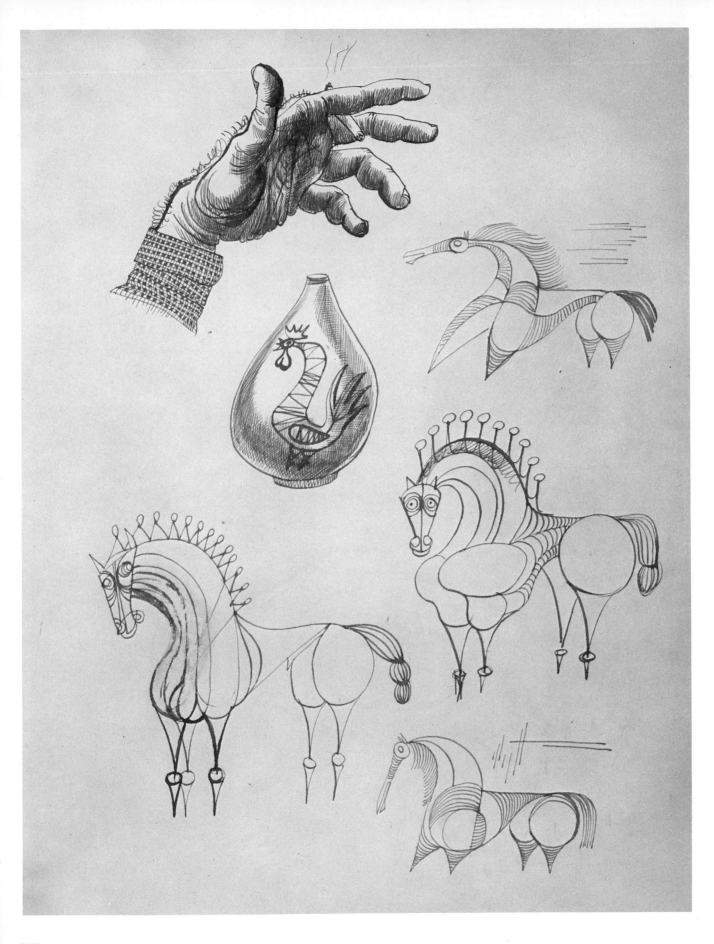

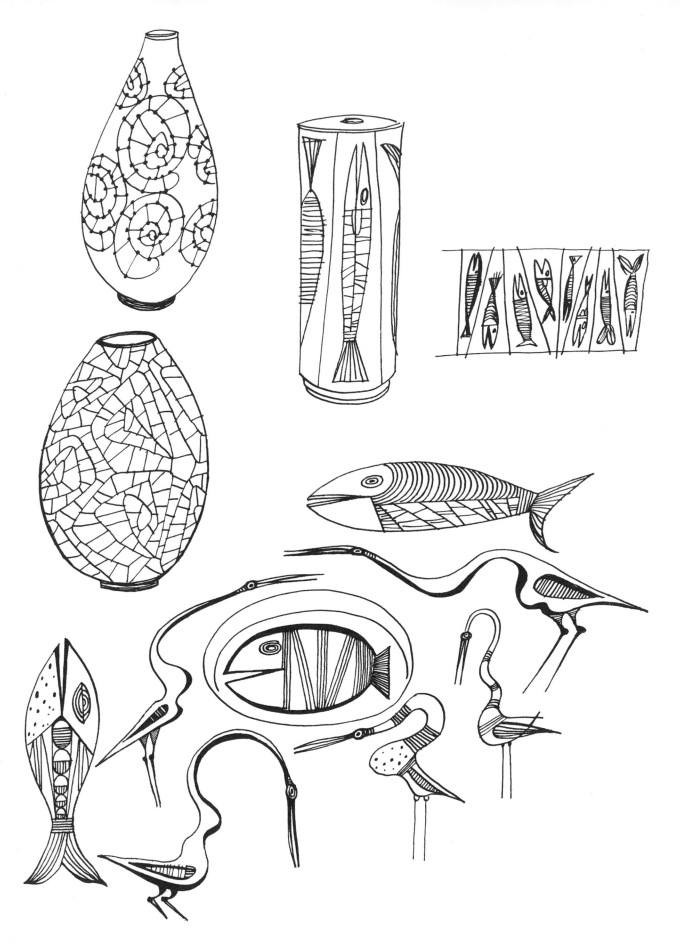

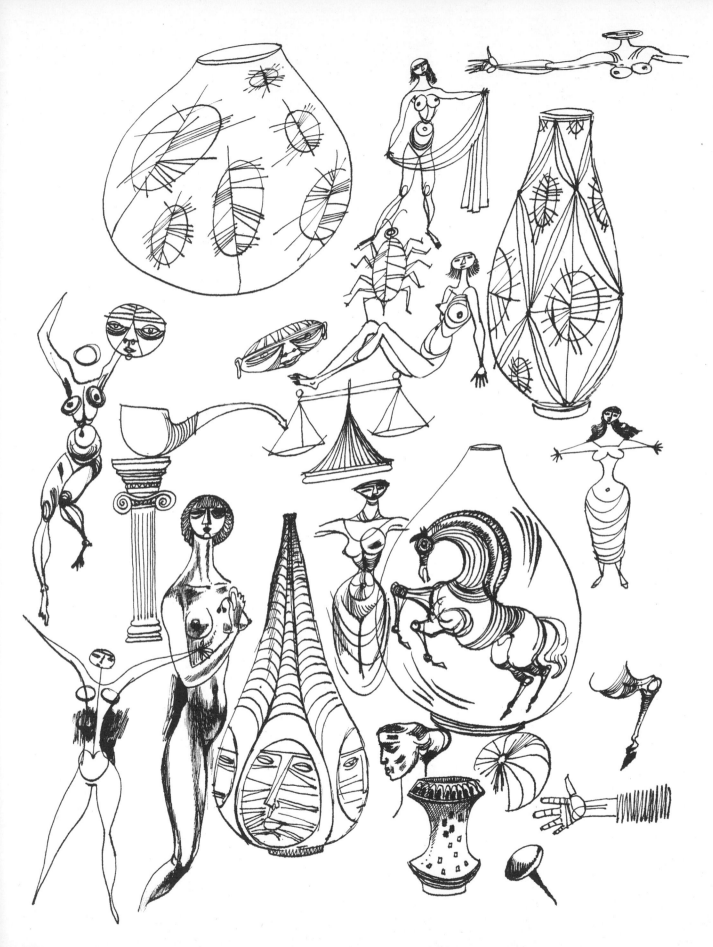

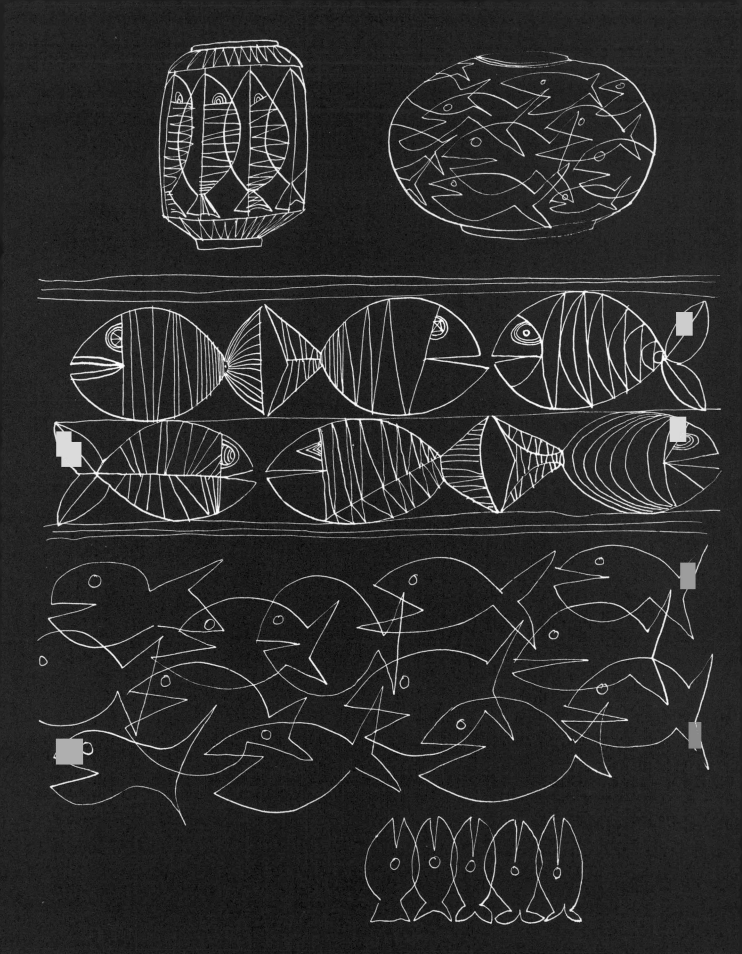

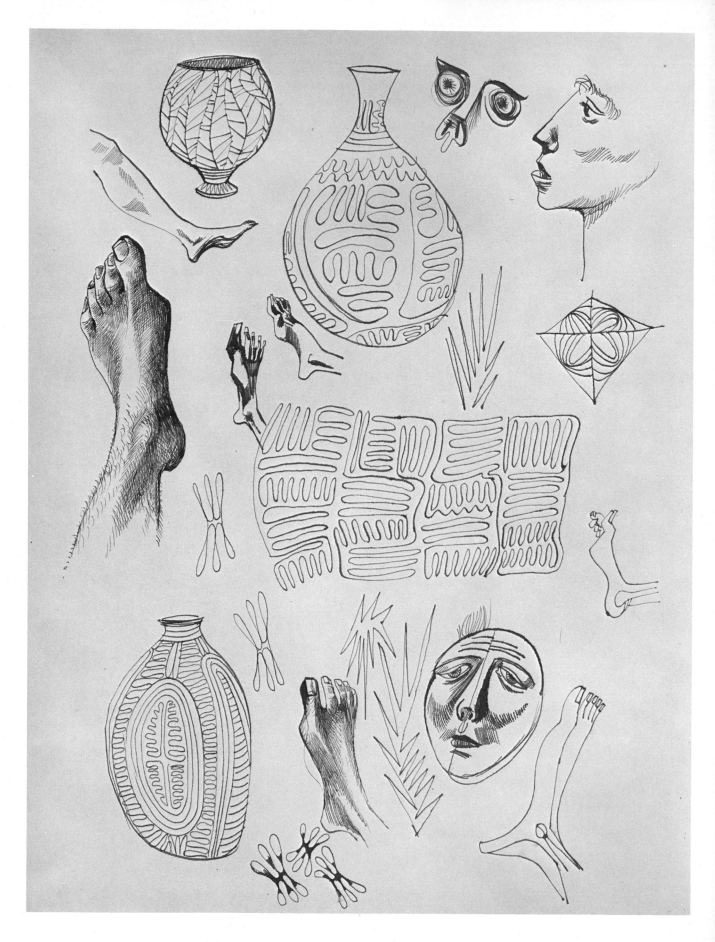

163

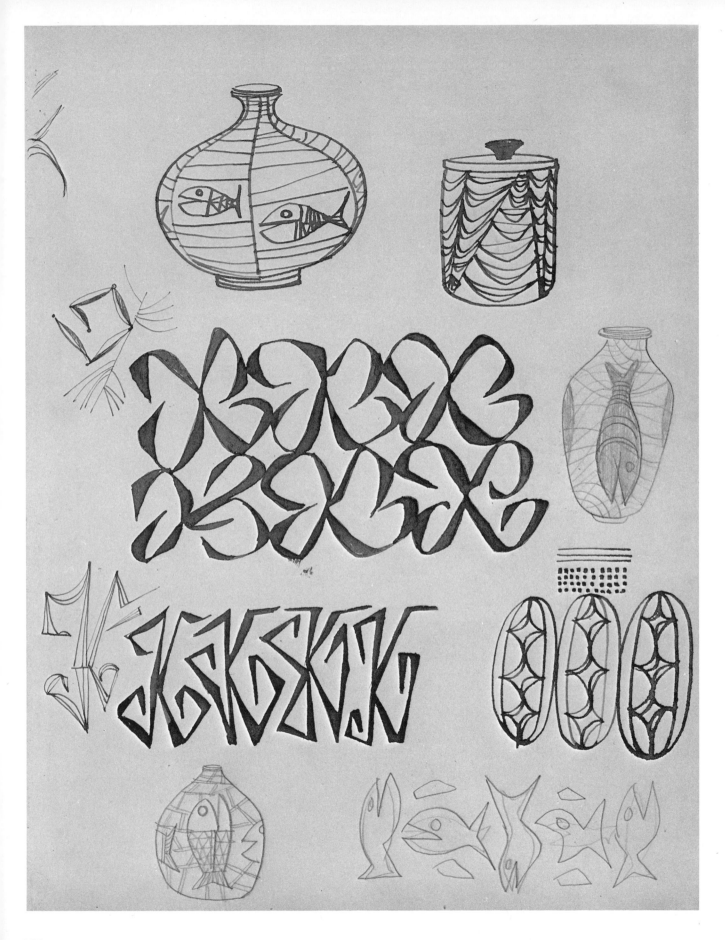

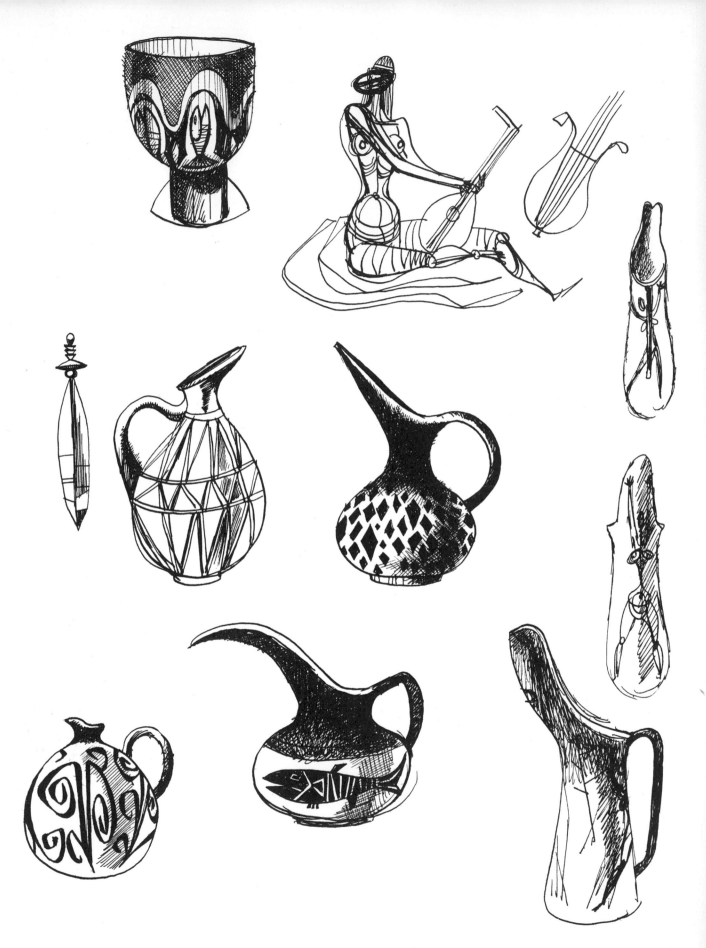

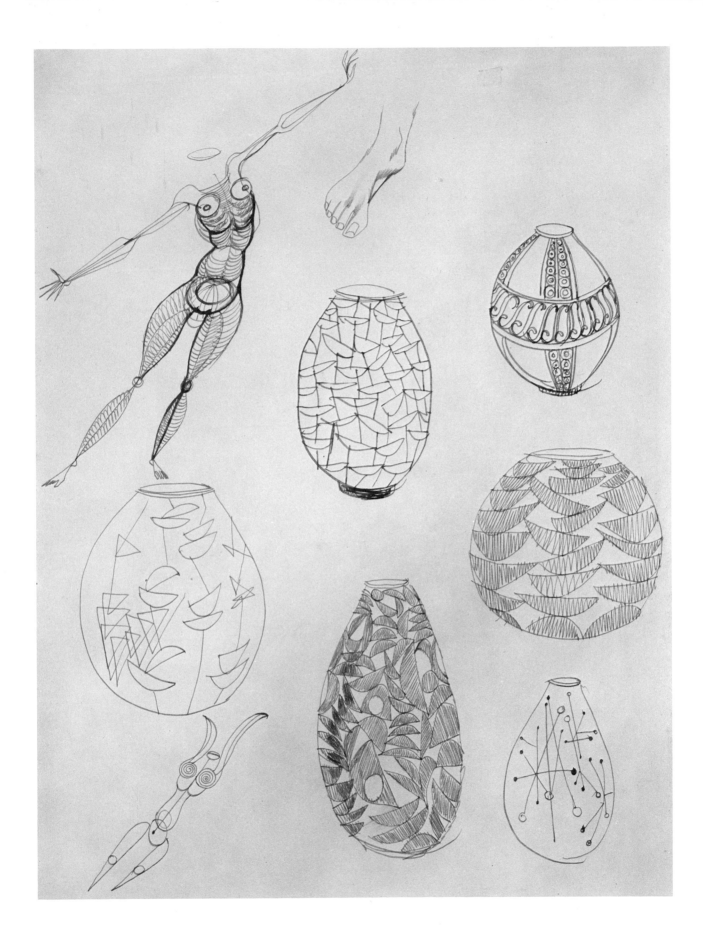

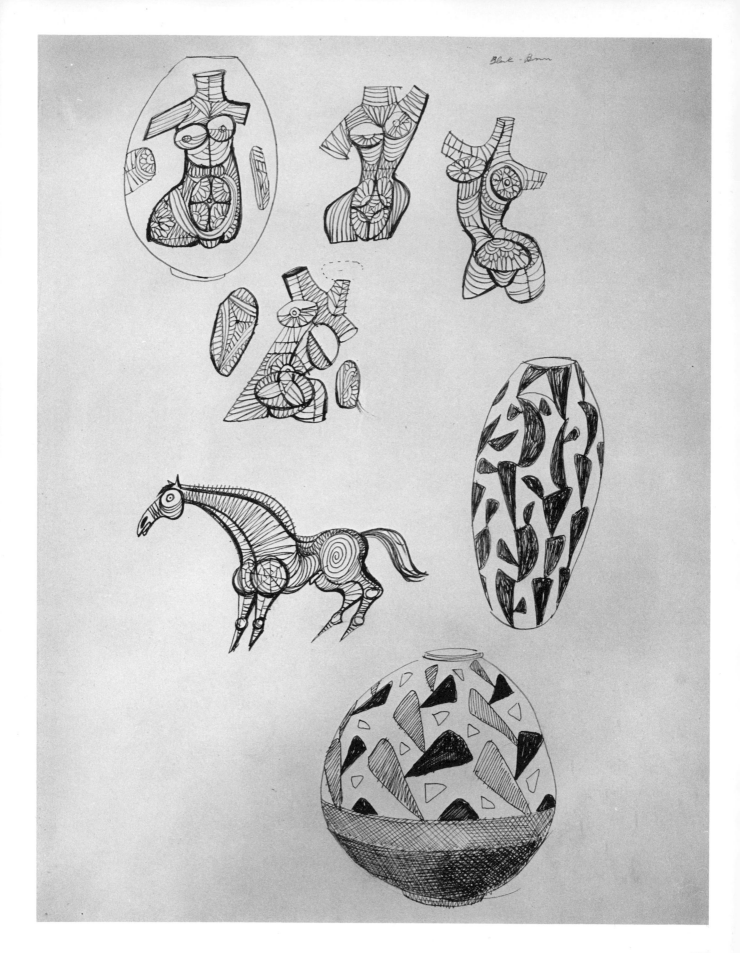

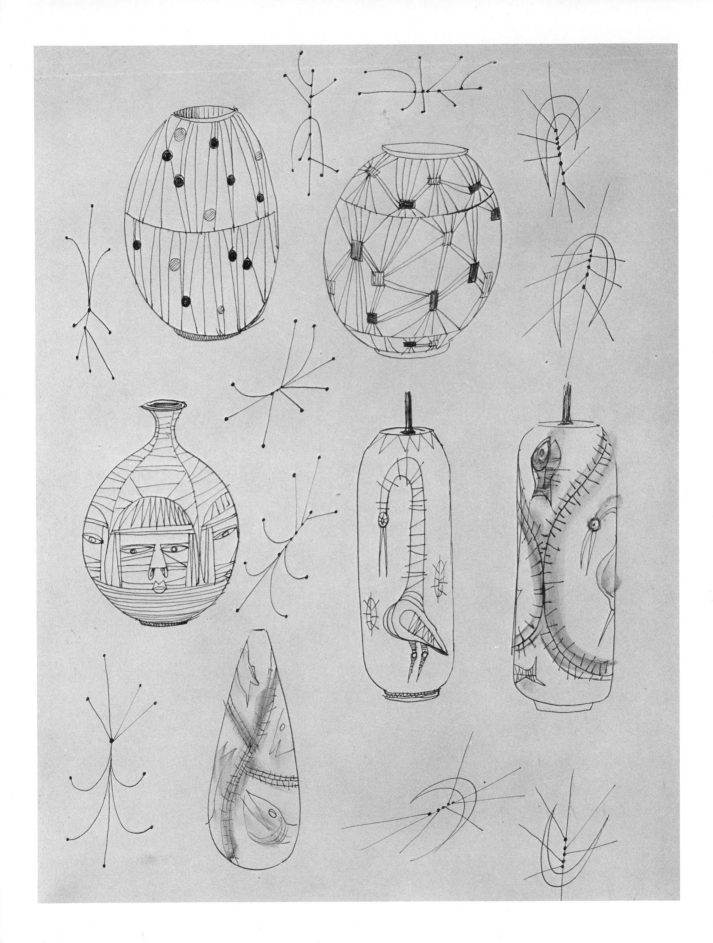

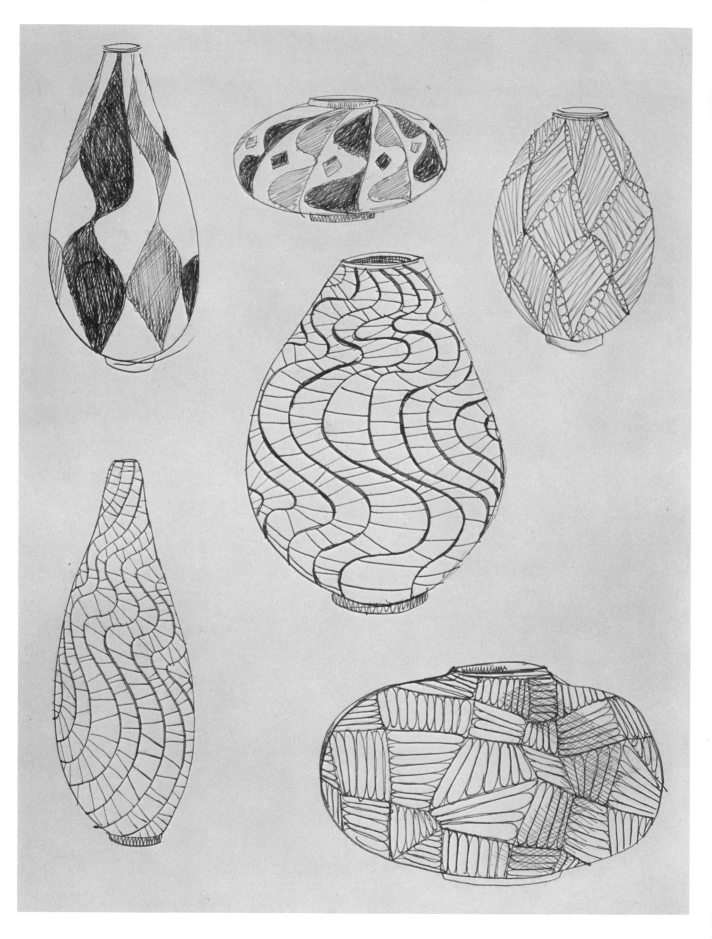

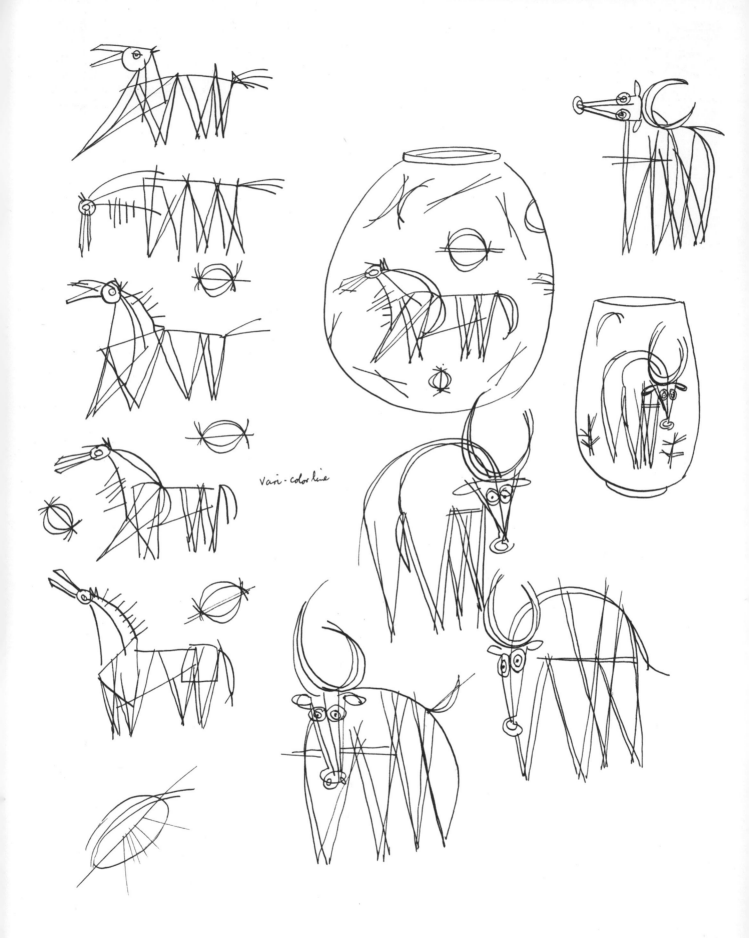

Vari-color line

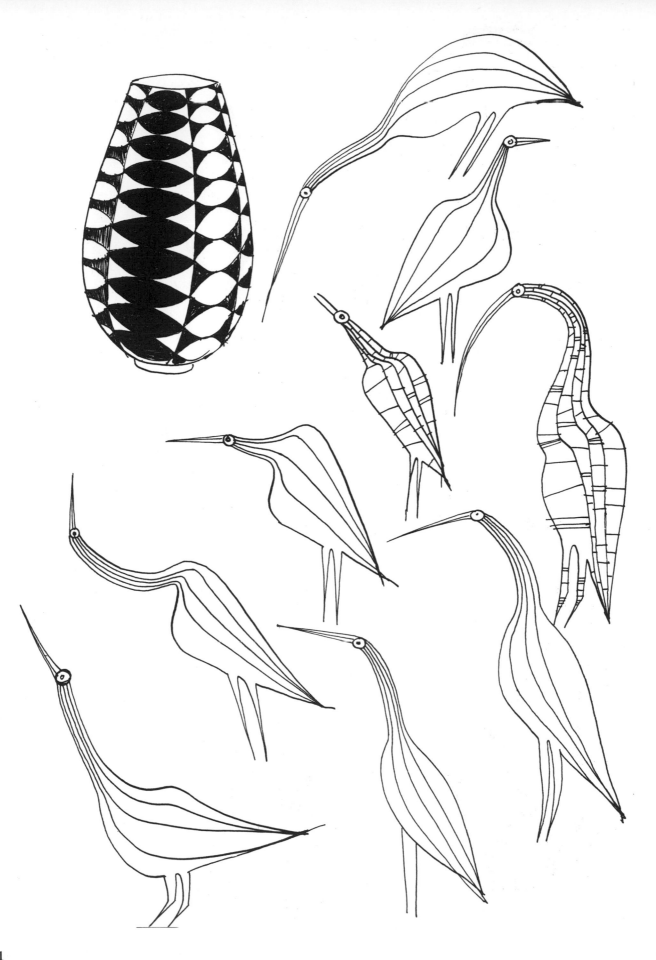

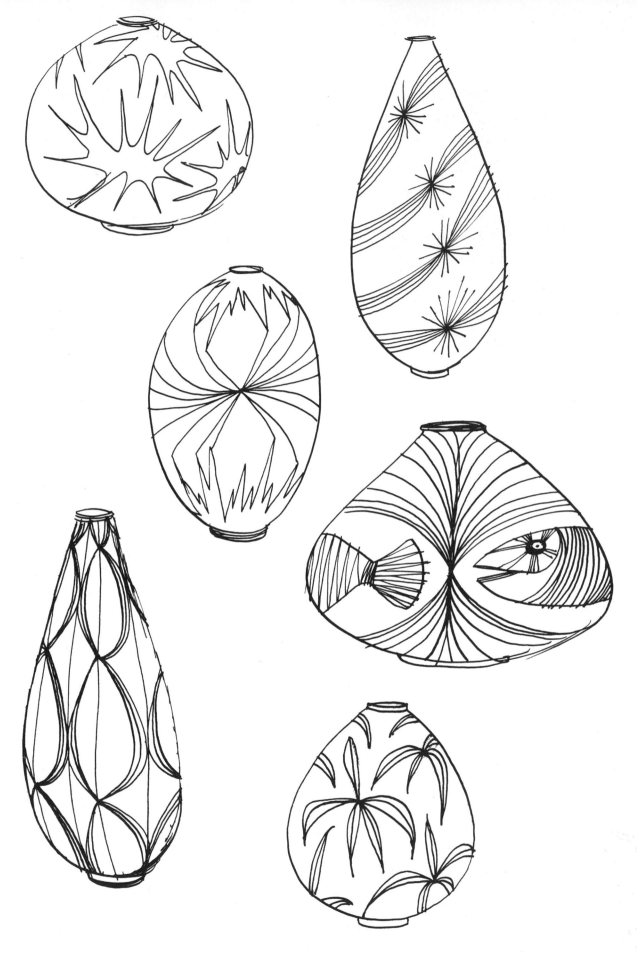

184

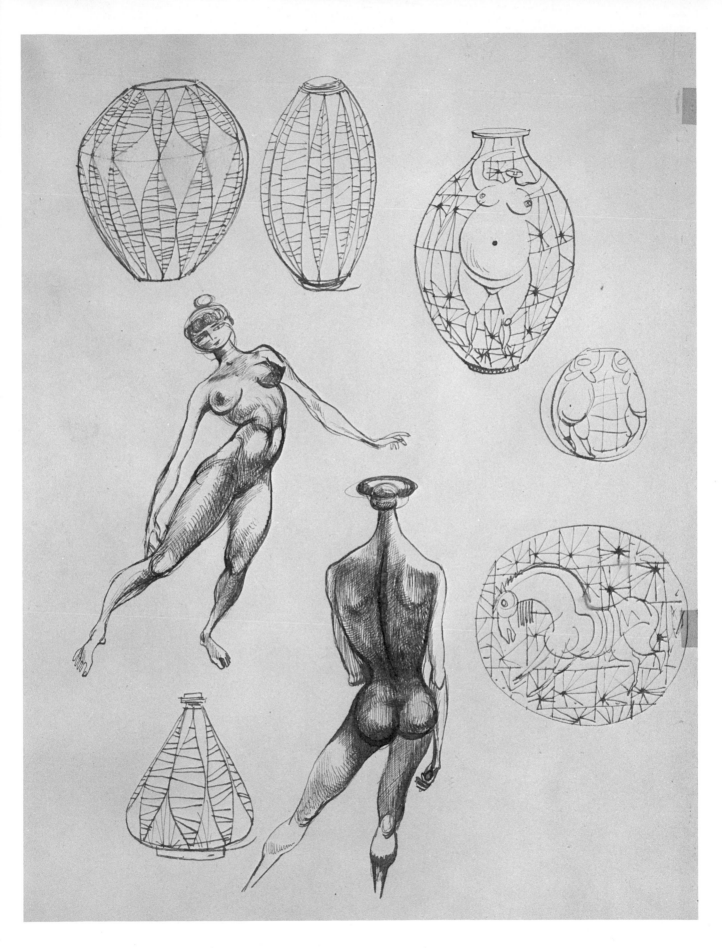

187

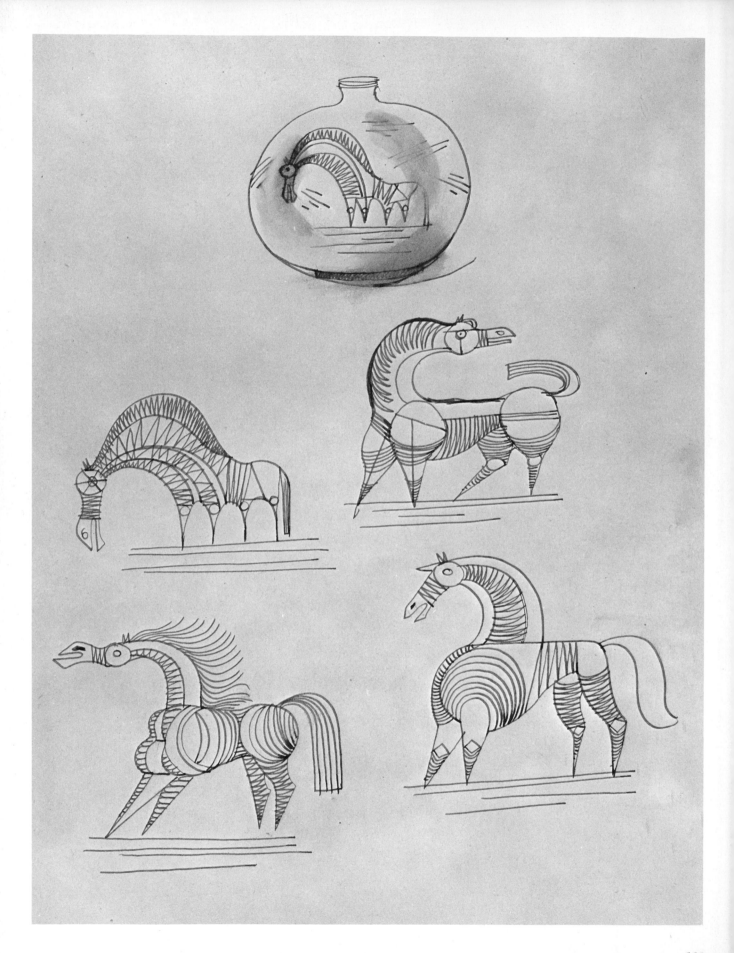

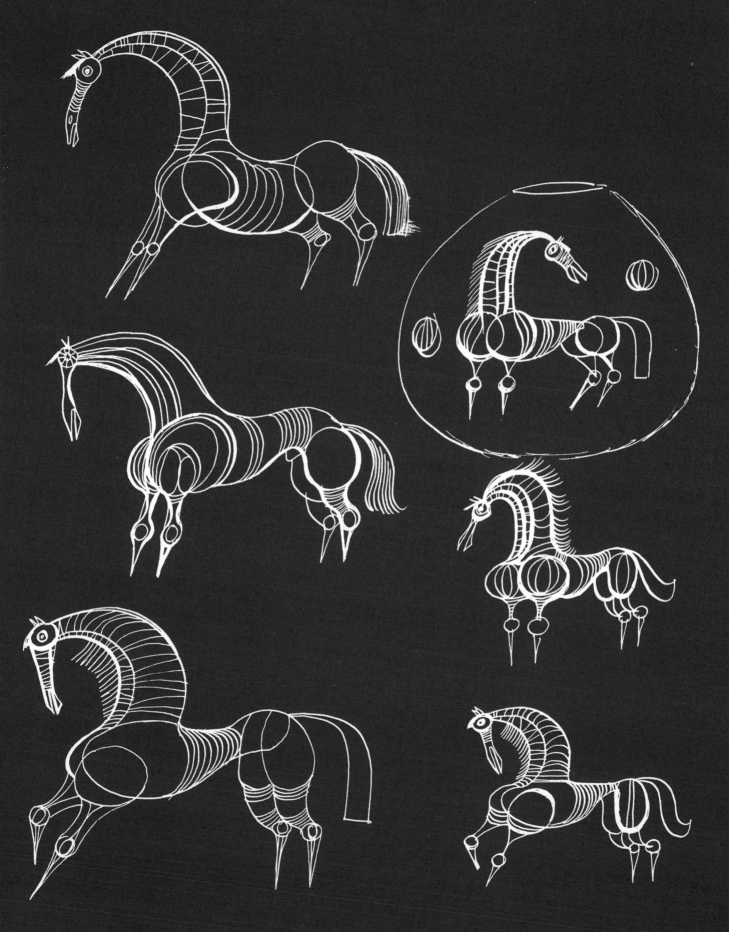

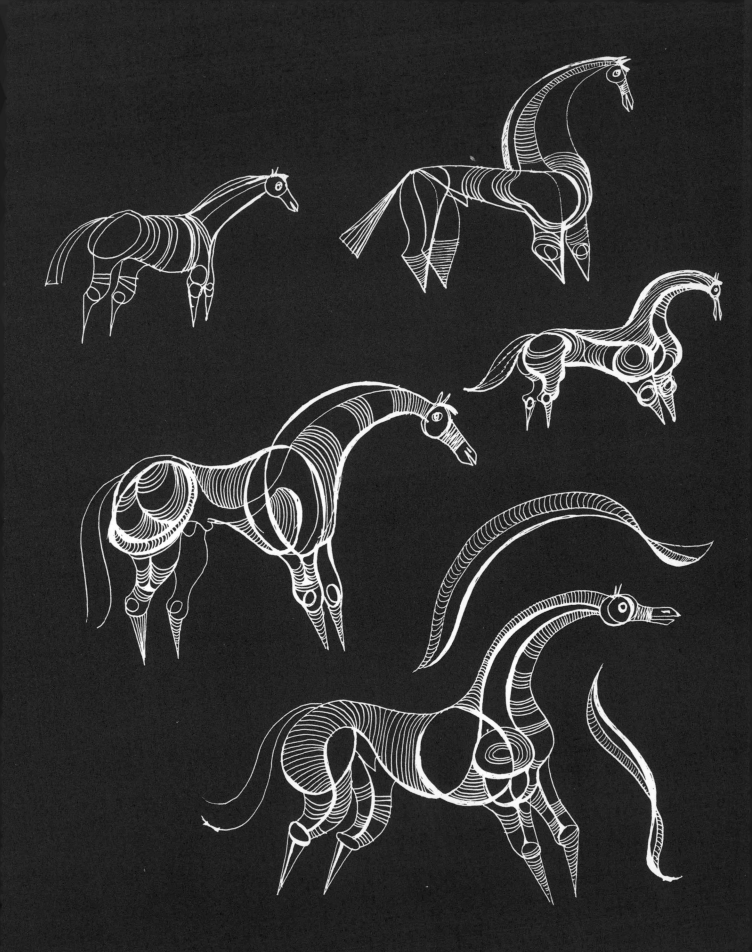

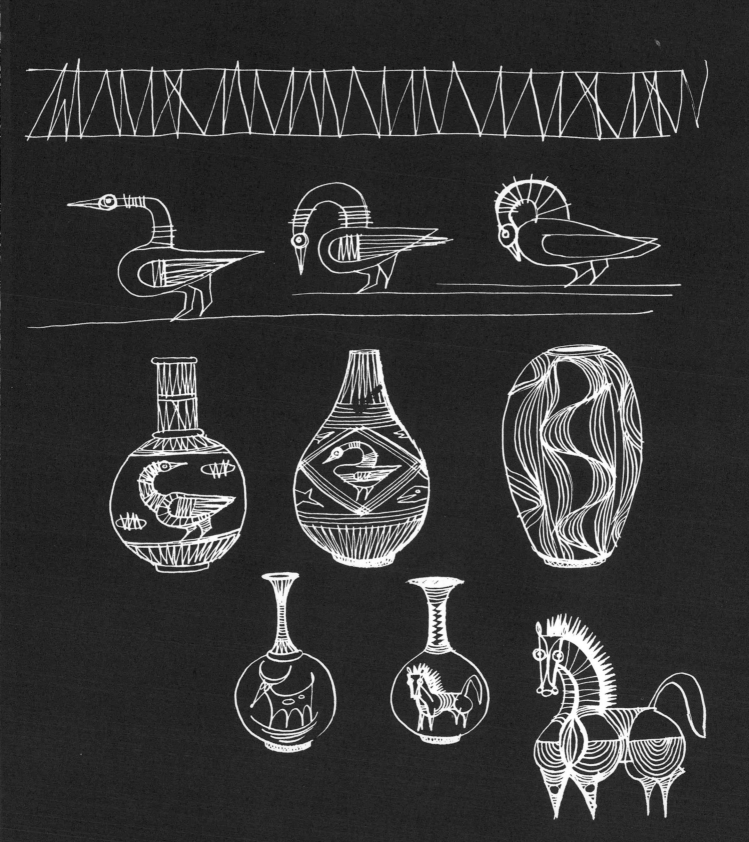

193

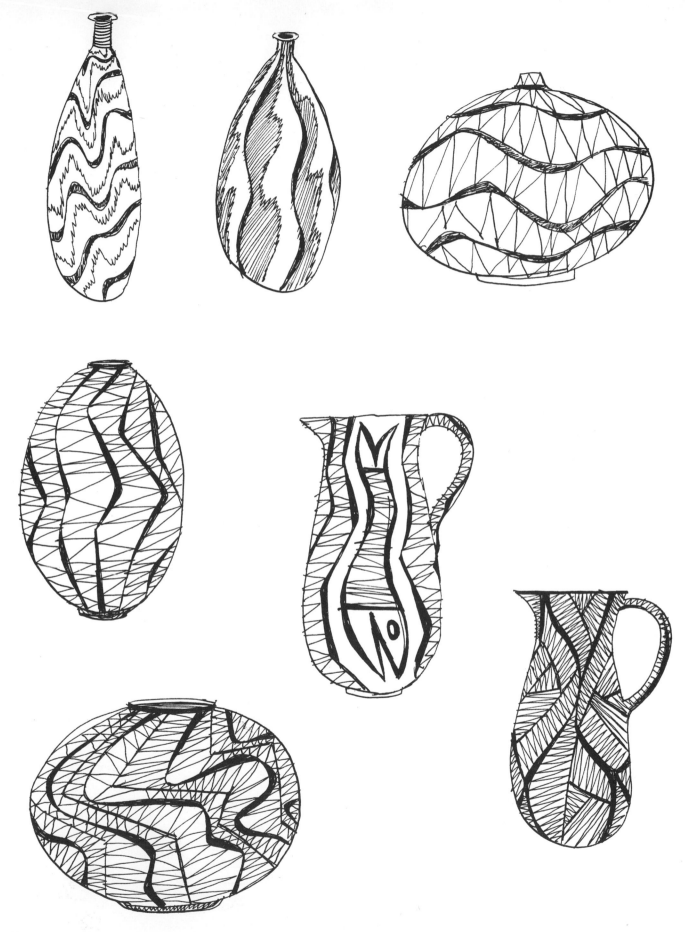

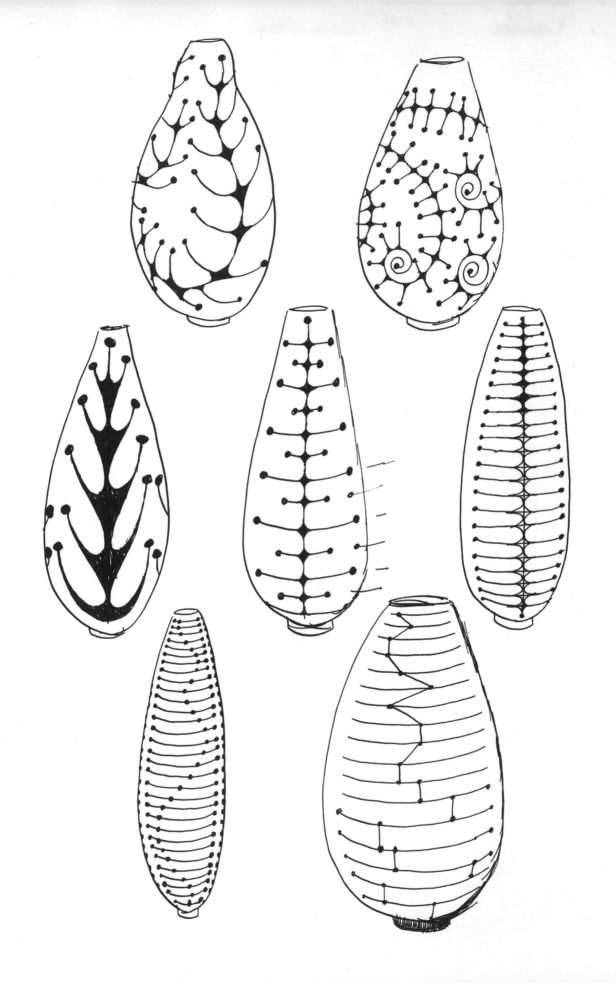